Personal Idealism and Mysticism

Paddock Lectures for 1906, Delivered at the General Seminary New York

By William Ralph Inge

PANTIANOS
CLASSICS

Published by Pantianos Classics

ISBN-13: 978-1-78987-476-1

First published in 1907

Contents

Preface

THESE Lectures were the occasion of my first visit to America, during which I made many friends, and experienced the wonderful hospitality and kindness which Americans, above all other nations, know how to show to visitors. The month which I spent in the United States will always be one of my happiest recollections.

The subject of the Lectures is far too wide to be dealt with satisfactorily in a short course. My purpose was rather to stimulate thought than to criticise a powerful school of philosophy and theology. Fortunately, the limitations of "Pragmatism" have been exposed by abler pens than mine; and it is to be hoped that its leading advocates will not allow themselves to be tempted away from psychology, where they are strong, to theology, where their influence appears to me to be mischievous. The term "Personal Idealism" has been selected by a group of these thinkers, to express their antagonism to Naturalism and Absolutism. The Preface to the volume of essays with this title is a lucid statement of the point of view against which these pages are directed.

W. R. I.

One – Our Knowledge of God

"SUCH as men themselves are, such will God appear to them to be." These words of John Smith, the Cambridge Platonist, state a primary fact about the conditions of religious belief from which we can no more escape than we can leap off our own shadows. The God of the moralist is before all things a great Judge and Schoolmaster; the God of the priest is the Head of the celestial and terrestrial hierarchies; the God of science is impersonal and inflexible vital Law; the God of the savage is the kind of chief he would be himself if he had the opportunity. So closely do gods resemble their worshippers that we might almost parody Pope's line and say that an honest God is the noblest work of man. This incurable anthropomorphism or anthropopsychism has been noticed and ridiculed from Xenophanes to Spinoza. It has been blamed, and to some extent justly, by prophetic writers. "Thou thoughtest wickedly," says the Psalmist, speaking to the ungodly in the name of Jehovah, "that I am even such an one as thyself." But the thoughts of the ungodly about God are only "wicked," because they are the thoughts of the ungodly. Our religion must be based upon our own experience, and it ought to be so. Although God's thoughts are not as our thoughts, nor His ways as our ways, we are made in His image, and no higher category than our own rational and spiritual life is open to us in which we could place Him. God has made us in His image, and we hope that we are in process of transformation into His likeness.

But what are "we"? Man is a microcosm, with affinities to every grade of God's creation. He is a little lower than the angels, and a little higher than the brutes. A modern biologist might wish to put it even more strongly. Every one of us, in his short span of life, recapitulates and hurries through the whole gamut of creation. In the nine months before we see the light, we pass through stages of evolution which in the race were spread over tens of millions of years. And in our upward progress i may there not be some dim anticipations of another long period of growth, which the slow mills of God are grinding out without haste and without rest? Can we set any limit to the achievements of human nature, which

God created to reflect His own, and which was revealed to half-blind eyes in its full potential dignity when the Word of God became flesh and tabernacled among us? We can only know what is akin to ourselves, but there is that in us which is akin to God Himself.

Is this mysterious centre of our being, this sacred hearth where the divine fire glows ever unextinguished, this eye which is "the same eye with which God sees us," to be regarded as a special organ or faculty of spiritual vision, apart from those faculties of which psychology takes cognisance intellect, will, and feeling? This does not seem to be the truth. There is no separate organ for the apprehension of divine truth, independent of will, feeling, and thought. Our knowledge of God comes to us in the interplay of those faculties. It is not given to us through any one of them acting apart from the others, nor indeed is it possible for any of them to act independently of the others. Our nature is not tripartite. "It is everywhere the whole mind, at once thinking, feeling, and passing moral judgments," says Lotze, "which out of the full completeness of its nature produces in us these unspoken first principles." Julian of Norwich says the same thing in simpler and nobler words: "Our faith cometh of the natural love of the soul, and of the clear light of our reason, and of the steadfast mind which we have of God in our first making."

We are thus united to God by all parts of our psychical nature a threefold cord which is not quickly broken. There is a Trinity within us, an indissoluble synthesis which nevertheless refuses to be wholly simplified, and which in our imperfect experience often appears as a concordia discors. For our nature is not fully attuned; there are contradictions, discords, strifes within and without, and these are reflected in the image which we are able to form of God. This is why so many who crave for peace, certainty, and definiteness, instead of accepting our appointed lot of struggle, faith, and hope, grasp at some delusive promise of a revelation communicated purely from without, as if such a revelation would carry with it some surer pledge of truth than the assent of our reason. But no such revelation could ever be made; for what part of ourselves could receive it? Are we asked to accept an incomprehensible truth because it is guaranteed by miracle? But what is the connection between the sign and the thing signified? Who shall convince us that there must be any connection at all? And if, as must needs be, the outward sign offers itself to our understanding only, how can the understanding, which deals with what is less than ourselves, prove the truth of what is above ourselves? No, the apparent externality of a revelation is no warrant of its divine character, or of its value. In proportion as a truth is external, it is either not revealed or not spiritual. For in the spiritual world there is no outside and inside. Spiritual things, as Plotinus says, are separated from each other not by local division, but only by discordance of nature. The organ by which we apprehend divine truth is no special faculty, but the higher reason, which we distinguish from the understanding because we mean it to include the will and feelings, disciplined under the guidance of the intellect. The higher reason is that unification of our personality which is the goal of our striving and the postulate of all our rational life. God is the last object to be clearly known, precisely because He is at once the presupposition and foundation and consummation of all our knowledge.

"The higher reason is king" (βασιλεὺς ὁ Νοῦς). I am not afraid to join Plotinus in this act of homage, in spite of all the heavy artillery which has been turned upon intellectualism in our generation, and nowhere with greater energy and effect than in the country of that brilliant psychologist, Professor William James. My position with regard to the claims of the intellect and the will to supremacy in religion must be explained, if I can succeed in explaining it, in my fifth lecture. Here I need only express my conviction that there are three avenues to the knowledge of God purposive action, reasoning thought, and loving affection; and that the normal order of their development is that in which I have put them. Their order of development, but not the order of their dignity. For the will may energise without either intelligence or affection; and the intellect may energise without affection, though not without the presence of will in the form of attention; but love in its divine fulness is the unity of will and reason in the highest power of each.

It is, I think, a strange thing that the religious psychology of the Neoplatonists, which through Augustine and others had such an immense influence upon Christian theology, should be so much neglected in our time. It is often supposed that Plotinus is only the chief European representative of a dreamy and unpractical type of philosophy which may be studied in its purest form in the Indian religions. But Neoplatonism is in the line of Greek, not Oriental, thought; and Plotinus is the last great figure in the magnificent series of Greek philosophers which spans the longest period of unfettered thought that the human race has ever been permitted to enjoy. The last word in philosophy of the old civilisation is not, as our English students are almost encouraged to believe, the proud and melancholy moralism of the later Stoics. The real conclusion of that long travail of thought was a system which expounds the philosophy of the soul's journey to God, as traversed in the normal religious experience. We find much the same chart in all the Christian mystics, not, for the most part, because they have read Plotinus, but because they have made the voyage for themselves. Such is, in point of fact, the road along which the soul must take its solitary journey. The map of the country is, as we might expect, drawn very much alike by all who have travelled through it.

In this introductory lecture I will try to give a sketch of the process by which, according to these authorities, and especially Plotinus, the father of European mysticism, we arrive at the knowledge of God. Keeping the old antithesis of the one and the many, which is as characteristic of Greek thought as insistence upon the subject-object relation is characteristic of modern philosophy, we may perhaps say that mere multiplicity - the πολλὰ μόνον - is the logical *reductio ad dbsurdum* of materialism, while bare abstract unity - the ἓν μόνον - is the *reductio ad absurdum* of idealism. These two extremes lie, for Neoplatonism, outside existence. The former is τὸ μὴ ὄν; of the latter it is said that "it is not" (οὐκ ἔστι), being beyond existence. Between them lie two spheres, of which the higher has for its principle the Intelligence (Νοῦς), the content of the Divine mind. Its numerical symbol is the One-Many (ἓν-πολλά). The One is manifested in a multiplicity of aspects, in which it appears polarised but not dissipated or even divided. For even as St. Augustine says of the omnipresence of God that He is not only present in all things, but present is His totality in all things, so Plotinus teaches that the whole is potentially present in each one of its parts. This "intelligible world" is the real world; in it God is immanent, and yet He is transcendent, because it is only as *His* thoughts and for His pleasure that the whole fair picture is outspread.

But the world in which we mostly live is not the intelligible world, the sphere of the OneMany, but the soul-world, of which the numerical symbol is the One and the Many (ἓν καὶ πολλά). To our normal consciousness, God the One is present, not as the unifying principle in all experience, but rather as the supreme Entity by the side of other entities, partially independent of Himself. There is in this sphere a partial disintegration of reality, a partial depotentiation of the Divine energy. It is in this sphere that evil asserts itself as the appearance of a positive force in rebellion against the will of God. The soul-world is also the time-world, for time (as Professor Royce has said) is the form of the will, and will or purposive action is the characteristic quality of the soul-life.

In what sense is the "soul-world" less real and less noble than the "intelligible world"? Was Plotinus at all misled by his favourite analogy of light, which is diminished by distance from its source and by the diffusion of its rays? Is not this an analogy which may fail in the spiritual world? And is there perhaps a trace of another fallacy, namely, that a state of change is inferior to and less divine than a state of immobility? Plotinus was well aware that "the eternal Now" (as Eckhart calls it), is not inertia but action viewed *sub specie aeternitatis*. His disciple Proclus distinguishes three kinds of *whole* - the sum of the parts, the resultant of the parts, and the contexture of the whole and its parts, which is the highest kind of unity. So St. Augustine says that things above are higher than things below, but that the whole creation together is higher than things above. This line of thought might suggest the conclusion that the sphere of the soul the will-world is not inferior to the intelligible world, but only to the supreme synthesis of will and intelligence in the Absolute' As a symbol of this synthesis we might use the old philosophical conception of an ἐνέργεια ἀκινησίας. Instead of an ascending series, we should then have the soul-world and the intelligible world in a kind of parallelism, with the ineffable One as the unknown but necessary reconciler and fulfiller of both. But this would not be a fruitful line of speculation. The parallelism between the physical and psychical must not be duplicated or interpreted as a parallelism between will and intelligence. The intelligible world, as envisaged by Plotinus, leaves out nothing that belongs to the world of soul, and must not be set in opposition to it. Its superiority lies in giving a positive value to elements which in the lower sphere appear as negations and discords - in finding a soul of goodness in things evil, and an eternal principle in the midst of time. Thus it involves the repudiation of that erroneous view - superficially optimistic but really pessimistic, which recognises no difference between that which is given in our normal experience and that which ought to be and must be. There are discords - there is evil - in the world of our common experience. The soul has its enemies, which in its own proper sphere must be hated, resisted, and overcome. But in the world of the eternal Ideas - God's own mind -

the victory is already won, and the bad transmuted or suppressed. And among the elements of that victorious good, in that world, are the energies which in the soul-life appear as effecting that result.

The intelligible world, then, is the sphere towards which we are ascending, and which is even now partly open to us. In this sphere, as I have said, God is both immanent and transcendent. Is this the final goal? To go beyond Intelligence, says Plotinus, is to fall outside it And yet, as we all know, the One beyond Intelligence plays an important part in his philosophy, and in the philosophy of mysticism generally. The Intellect, even in its most exalted and comprehensive significance, even the Νοῦς ἐρῶν, the *Amor intellectualis Dei,* is not allowed to have quite the last word. Even as religion starts in an undifferentiated feeling of the Beyond, a feeling in which all possible developments of the moral, intellectual, and emotional life are implicit, so its supreme and ideal consummation, after the wheel has gone full circle, must be a final identification of thinker and thought, in which the Mind, which has come to its full rights by including all experience within itself, passes again on an infinitely higher plane into the region of undifferentiated feeling. The extremes are simple, says Proclus, the intermediate stages complex. So Clement of Alexandria tells us that faith, the first stage of our course, and love, the last, "are not taught": there is a spontaneity in them which is lacking in the long day's work. Platonism and Christianity are at one in representing the final consummation as a passing of knowledge into love. The "intellect in love" loses itself in the supreme transit which is its goal and the end of its labours.

Logically, the system is incomplete without this ideal completion of the spiritual ascent, though it has but little relation to any facts of experience. Love the unifier is ours; but to be "made perfect in love" belongs not to our present state. It is more than doubtful whether the ecstasy, which the mystics valued as an anticipation of the beatific vision, is anything more than a proof of the wise maxim already quoted, that to strive to pass beyond reason is to fall outside it. Medical psychology has not yet fully explained the religious ecstasy, and I will not attempt to discuss what parts in it should be assigned to unconscious cerebration, to nervous exhaustion following on emotional overstrain, and to genuine illumination. The question whether, on mystical principles, we can know God without at least occasionally swooning into the Absolute, must be answered by drawing, with Eckhart, a distinction between the Godhead and God. Our knowledge must be of God, not of the Godhead, and the God of religion is not the Absolute, but the highest form under which the Absolute can manifest Himself to finite creatures in various stages of imperfection. The God of religion is not the Father of lights with whom is no variableness, for life without change is a state of which we have no experience, but the Father revealed by the Son. "No man hath seen God at any time. The only-begotten Son, who is in the bosom of the Father, He hath declared Him."

The ethical system which corresponds to this philosophy of religion is not, as is often supposed, dreamy or unpractical. The so-called civic virtues are placed by Plotinus at the bottom of the scale, not at all to disparage them, but because they must be practised by all, though all are not called to contemplation. Next to them come the cathartic virtues, by which our characters are purified. When a man has advanced as far as this, he is an efficient and useful member of society, and he has acquired self-control. Intellectually, his discipline has impressed upon him just those facts about God which those who aspire to be mystics without going through it never perceive. He has learned that God is *not* "the Infinite" that, on the contrary, He is known to us as the Principle of order and limitation (τάξις and πέρας). He has learned that "all's Law," as he will some day learn that "all's Love." His experience so far has been definite and concrete. He has learned *quid possit oriri, quid nequeat;* he has no love for the "loose types of things through all degrees" which fascinate the shallow pseudo-mystic; he knows the value of sharp outlines, and the importance of exact information. He has also learned the great lesson that illumination is not granted to the mere thinker, but to him who acts while he thinks, and thinks while he acts. Lastly, he knows the meaning of *sin*. No one can try to purify himself even as God is pure, without knowing the meaning and power of sin.

But this severe mental and moral discipline brings its reward in its own partial supersession. Dualism is, after all, appearance and not reality. Apparent contradictions in the nature of things, when faced perfectly fairly, can be lived down. And so the inner discord of flesh and spirit is attuned, and even sin itself, whether in ourselves or in the world, is partly seen to be "behovable," as Julian of Norwich says. The will, no longer divided against itself, passes into intelligence; we become fellow-workers with God, rather than day labourers in His service. The broken images of order and beauty, which we have trained ourselves to observe and reverence in the world, begin to form themselves into a glorious universe of gracious design, through which the Divine Wisdom passes and penetrates, mightily and sweetly ordering all things.

The human soul leaps forward to greet this vision of glory and harmony, as a child recognises and greets his father's house. It is at home there; this is the heaven in which it was meant to dwell. Meanwhile, the virtues which it learned at the earlier stages are still practised, but without the old strain. They have become habitual; and the approving intellect now holds the reins instead of the struggling will. And when at last love suffuses all the mind - love of God and His laws, and love for our neighbour as made in His image, and the chief mirror of His goodness, then indeed the yoke becomes easy and the burden light. "The toil and sweat of virtue," says Hesiod, "the immortal gods have set at the beginning of the journey; long and hard and rough is the path that leads thereto, at first; but when we reach the top, then indeed it becomes easy, though hard."

Such is the general scheme of the "Scale of Perfection" as accepted by the Neoplatonists, and by the Christian mystics who owed so much to them. I do not think that it is out of date, nor that it ever will be out of date.

A very important question may here suggest itself. Is the ascent purely and exclusively ethical? Does the fifteenth psalm give us all the conditions under which a man may ascend unto the hill of the Lord? We may be content to follow Plotinus in using "the Good" as another name for the supreme category which he calls the One, though strictly speaking the Absolute must be beyond the Good which we contrast with the Bad. But, though it perhaps requires some courage to say so, I do not think that we have any right to assume that God is a purely ethical Being. The. True and the Beautiful seem also to be roads up the hill! of the Lord, as well as the Good; and though i we are fully convinced that they all meet at the top, we are doing considerable violence to parts of our experience if we determine rigorously that God can have no other motive in His creation except a purely ethical one. Much of nature's plan impresses us as a work of sublime intellect and ingenuity, but not as a scheme in which these are wholly subordinated to moral evolution. And is it not more than probable, judging from what we see around us, that *beauty* also must be an end in itself to the Creator of our universe? It seems to me that Truth and Beauty are ideals too august to be ever regarded as means only. Science and Art are both false to themselves if they suffer themselves to be mere handmaids of morality. Writers on religion and morals generally regard it as a point of honour to prove that conduct is the whole of life, as if any other interest was unworthy of God. But if a large measure of intellectual and aesthetic interest is a worthy ingredient in the highest human character, if it is an enrichment and adornment enhancing the value of the most saintly life, why should not the same qualities, infinitely magnified, and exalted above all impurities and imperfections, hold a place in the character of God Himself? I do not see why they should not; and I see many reasons for thinking that they actually do. The kind of ethical obsession which dominates many religious thinkers is, in my opinion, the cause of errors and defects in their view of life.

I believe that the determination to find in God's government of the world the rule of a moralist pure and simple has been a great obstacle to understanding the actual laws under which we live. These laws, we must believe, contain nothing *contrary* to the moral goodness of the Creator; but I repeat that I can see nothing derogatory to the character of God in supposing that other considerations, besides those which we call moral, have entered into their texture. If so, it is our duty to study reverently that most wonderful mechanism, that complex yet harmonious wisdom which is manifested alike in the infinitely great and the infinitesimally small, and we shall recognise cheerfully that scientific ignorance, as well as moral turpitude, deserves and will suffer God's displeasure. It is easy to see what a large part of the problem of Divine justice receives here a solution which the mere moralist is precluded from offering. It is also clear that, if we are right, the scientific investigator should be given an honoured place among the priests and prophets. He should work as a servant of God, and should be recognised as such. The metaphysician should work in the same spirit, and should receive the same reverence. "Mein liebe Frau, das Denken ist auch Gottesdienst," as Hegel said to his housekeeper. I think that this is a truth which needs to be urged at the present time, especially as regards the natural sciences. We are living just after a real *fin de siècle* - the end of one of the most remarkable epochs since the human race began its course. The nineteenth century cannot, perhaps, claim the foremost place for brilliancy of imagination or keenness of insight; but it gave mankind for the first time a firm grasp on the continuity and unity of nature, and it reaped a rich harvest in applying this hypothesis to scientific investigation. "The scientific mind," says Merz, in his interesting book, *The History of European Thought in the Nineteenth Century,* "advances from the idea of order or arrangement to that of unity, through the idea of continuity." This reminds us of Plotinus' claim that the study of nature and the practice of social virtues teach us the place of τάξις and πέρας in God's world. That these intellectual discoveries have a moral and religious significance is well shown by the same author. "The reason," he says, "why the concepts of order and unity have received so much attention lies in this, that they have not only a logical meaning as instruments, but also, as the words themselves indicate, a practical meaning, being bound up with the highest ethical and aesthetical, as well as with our social and religious interests."

One would have supposed that this particular avenue to the knowledge of God would have been trodden by many religious thinkers in our generation. But it is not so. The over-confidence and optimism of the great scientists in the middle of the nineteenth century have been followed by a vehement reaction against the religion of nature. It is almost denied that nature bears any impress of the Creator's character. "Considered apart from its relation to the moral and religious life of the subject," says Tyrrell, who in this passage speaks for a large class of thinkers, "the world is stamped with no more than a footprint of the Divinity - with a sign that He was once there and has passed by. It shows a limited and unconscious intelligence and purpose, such as a mechanism might owe to the past creative act of its contriver. Its goodness and wisdom are but caricatures of the Divine, blasphemous because of their very traces of likeness; mimicking the Creator as a marionette mimicks its living maker. Nor must we be deceived by the vast scale on which these traces are manifested; for if there are signs of an intelligence and benevolence beyond all possible measure of human capacity, these are more than cancelled by the scale on which failure in both respects is apparent. If no man could be so good or wise as nature seems, neither could any man be so cruel or so wanton. Only in goodness of character have we anything that may reverently be called an image of the indwelling goodness of God. The conception of nature as being, apart from man, a direct expression or self-manifestation of the Divine character, is responsible for the moral and spiritual perversions that are everywhere associated with polytheistic or pantheistic nature-worship. To worship the caricature of Divinity there revealed to us is really to worship the Devil." [1] Now there is an ambiguity in this phrase about worshipping nature apart from man. Assuredly man is part of nature, and if we wish to pronounce judgment on the mercy or justice of nature's methods, we are bound to take into consideration that mercy and justice are honoured, and often practised, in one part of nature, namely, that part in which alone the claim for them is understood. Nature includes man, and man at his best. Nature includes the best man that ever lived - it includes the divine life on earth of Jesus Christ. When, therefore, it is declared that nature, as revealed to us by science, including man as known to anthropology, is a godless, even a devilish system, which can only become worthy of respect when translated somehow into the categories of the "will-world," and so transformed and moralised throughout, we are exercising a right which leads to disaster even in the "will-world," and which is not recognised in the world of reason - the right to be wilful. We have no licence to rebuild the world of experience in accordance with our shallow notions of what ought to be. If our notions of morality conflict with the known laws of the universe, it is not always the laws which have to be changed. Tyrrell's tirade against naturalism seems to involve him first in deism, when he speaks of such limited intelligence as a mechanism might owe to the past creative act of its contriver, and then in Manicheism, when he seems ready to hand over the natural order to the devil. This last notion finds an unexpected supporter in Huxley, who in his well-known Romanes Lecture regards man's highest ethical ideals and the cosmic process as hopelessly antagonistic a view which implies either that God is divided against Hunself, or that the God of nature is the enemy of the God of conscience. If this were a true account of the matter, the world would indeed be a moral chaos. Another statement, of the same tendency, and almost equally unsatisfactory; is that nature is merely a system of *instruments,* having no independent existence or reality, but designed to be used by personal spirits for their own ends. But the proposed line between spirits and instruments, wherever we draw it, must be purely arbitrary and artificial. Science knows no such demarcation. Science and sound philosophy teach us that all nature is of one piece, animated in various degrees by one and the self -same spirit and obeying the self-same laws.

Lotze, from whom, in spite of his efforts to arrive at a monistic conclusion, much of this pluralistic "will-philosophy" is derived, is equally unsympathetic with regard to the approach to God through the appreciation of beauty. In flat contradiction to all Platonists, he holds that the reality of the external world is utterly severed from our senses. It is vain, he says, to call the eye sun-like, as if it needed a special occult power to copy what it has itself produced: "fruitless are all mystic efforts to restore to the intuitions of sense, by means of a secret identity of mind with things, a reality outside ourselves." In proof, he suggests that mountaineers are not, in point of fact, conspicuous for the broad and rich spiritual interests which the habitual contemplation of nature's grandest scenes might (on Plato's theory) have been expected to produce. He protests against the notion that nature has any symbolic value; if it has suggestions to offer in the sphere of conduct, they are, he thinks, not very moral ones. For my own part, I believe that the Platonists and Wordsworth are right, and Lotze wrong. I agree with Scotus Erigena that "every visible and invisible creature is a theophany," and with Charles Kingsley that "all symmetrical natural objects are types of some spiritual truth and existence." I hold no brief for the so-called "mysticism" which arouses the ire of writers like Max Nordau. I have already disclaimed any sympathy with fanciful symbolism, as being above all else alien to the true spirit of mysticism. We must treat fact with the utmost reverence, and merely subjective interpretations of fact with a wholesome scepticism. But the approach to God through beauty, whether in nature or art, is not in any way hampered by this caution. For though the ideals of truth and beauty may seem like rivals, as being alike universal in their claims, and demanding a wholly disinterested mind in their respective worshippers, they clash with each other singularly little, less than either of them does with the moral ideal, and they help each other in many ways. I believe, then, that the moral consciousness is not the only faculty by which we apprehend God, but that the laws of nature and the beauty of the external world are also revelations of His being and character.

What, now, is the general character of the revelation of God which is made to us along these three lines? By "revelation" I understand, with Emerson, "the announcements of the soul, its manifestations of its own nature." "This communication," he says, "which is always attended by an emotion of the sublime, is an influx of the Divine mind into our mind...By the necessity of our constitution a certain enthusiasm attends the individual's consciousness of that Divine presence. The character and duration of this enthusiasm varies with the state of the individual, from the ecstasy of prophetic inspiration to the faintest glow of virtuous emotion." The consciousness of God is always accompanied by a stirring of the soul's inmost depths, whether it is aroused by the operation of the will, intellect, or aesthetic feelings. Religious utterance, therefore, has always a poetic or prophetic character. A hymn like the *Te Deum* is a better expression of the Christian faith than the Athanasian or even the Nicene Creed. But since the realisation of God's presence is always fitful and difficult, nothing in the least like a scheme of theology is given intuitively. This latter is the creation of the imaginative intelligence, which has to form out of its prior experience some picture, idea, or history of the world, to which the religious conviction may correspond, and in which its activity may find scope. Parts of the framework may afterwards prove to be unsound and to need reconstruction. In this sense it is permissible to say that illusion has played an important part in the history of religious belief. Such illusions have been the nationalism of the old Hebraic religion, and the belief of the early Christians in the approaching return of Christ in glory. In secular history, various enthusiasms, patriotic and political, have been illusions of the same kind. So much we must admit. But when some thinkers go further than this, and assert that religious truth is "poetic" in the sense that its objective correspondence with fact is a matter of indifference, we cannot agree. Such writers as Comte and Lange seem to think that mere ideals, which are not even supposed to correspond with any reality, are enough to sustain religious faith and zeal. But this is obviously to confound religion and poetry, which are quite different things. We can appreciate the Epic and Tragic poetry of the Greeks as much as if we believed that Polyphemus, Prometheus, and Medea were real persons; but we cannot any longer value a religious dogma which we have come to believe to be only a figment of the imagination. It would be hardly worth asserting, if it had not been so often questioned, that religious belief claims objective truth for the articles of its creed, and cannot continue to hold them if it is obliged to give up their objective truth. And yet this belief in the objective truth of our beliefs may - I had almost said must - have a psychological basis. For instance, I hope to show that the concrete monotheism of our Trinitarian doctrine is not less, but more worthy of acceptance, because we can find what Julian of Norwich calls "a made Trinity, like the unmade blessed Trinity," in our own souls. For that very reason, we cannot explain it to ourselves. We are unable to conceive clearly of a Being in whom Power, Wisdom, and Goodness are one, because this unification is still an unrealised ideal in ourselves, nor can we see it fully realised in the world around us. The doctrine must therefore remain a "mystery" to us, that is, a truth which we can apprehend but not comprehend, a truth which we can only represent by means of inadequate symbols.

The importance of Trinitarian doctrine centres in the question, What think ye of Christ? The opponents of mysticism, and especially of mysticism in its Platonic or "Alexandrian" form, have made the most of the charge that this type of Christianity refuses to know Christ after the flesh, and ultimately leaves Him behind altogether. I wish to deal with this charge, and with the question how far the doctrine of the Incarnate Logos has a permanent value for Christian philosophy.

I must also deal with the problem of personality, and with the question whether the God of Christianity is finite and relative, a Spirit among other spirits, or the "All in all," the Absolute. In this introductory lecture it will be enough to point out that the psychological basis of both problems is apparent. It is because our personality is limited and contingent that we find it easier to believe in a God than in God. I agree with Tyrrell that "the fiction of God's finitude and relativity is a necessity of man's religious life, but that the interests both of intellectual truth and of religion require us to recognise this fiction as such, under pain of mental incoherence on one side and of superstition and idolatry on the other." Acceptance of the finitude of God is closely connected with the volitive psychology, and with the rigorous moralism which we have seen to be frequently joined with it. It is the conscience in her struggle with evil that demands a God seriously engaged in the same conflict. Perhaps we may say that the notion of a finite God is one that the moralist can never afford to forget, nor the metaphysician to remember.

Lastly, the problem of Sin is one which a sympathiser with mysticism cannot honestly omit, just because it is the most difficult for him to deal with. The "problem of evil" is manifestly insoluble; we have to make our choice between theories, none of which is free from grave difficulties and objections. But the religious problem of Sin has in our day entered upon new phases, partly in response to what seems to me a remarkable change in the feeling about moral guilt and punishment among religious people, and partly as the result of new views about Inspiration, affecting the value attached to the narrative of the Fall.

My object in these lectures is quite frankly to urge the claims of what may be shortly called Christian Platonism, as a corrective to certain tendencies in modern thought which I regret. Truth has many sides; and even those who do not agree with me will perhaps sympathise with my anxiety that certain very beautiful hues in the "many-coloured wisdom of God" shall not be lost to our generation.

[1] *Lex Orandi*, p. 145.

Two - Sources and Growth of the Logoschristology

The doctrine of the Trinity in the New Testament may be best understood by collecting the passages which speak of the Divine indwelling in the human soul. Jesus Christ came to earth to reveal the Father, and the Holy Ghost came to reveal the Son. Nevertheless, there is no question of a dynasty in three reigns, that of the Father before the Incarnation, that of the Son during the Incarnation, and that of the Holy Ghost from Pentecost onwards. Neither the Son nor the Holy Ghost "speaks of Himself." The Son is the "Word" of the Father, and the Holy Ghost, in our Lord's words, "shall take of mine and shall show it unto you." So in St. Paul, we find the Divine immanence in the soul of the spiritual Christian spoken of quite indifferently as the indwelling of God, of Christ, of the Spirit of God, of the Spirit of Christ, and of the Spirit. In one passage [1] we have what is really a formal identification, as regards their operations, of the glorified Christ and the Holy Ghost. "The Lord is the Spirit," we read, "and where the Spirit of the Lord is, there is liberty." Bengel's words, "*conversio fit ad Dominum ut Spiritum*," are therefore thoroughly Pauline.

Our modern conceptions of *personality,* alien even to Roman, much more to Greek thought, have created difficulties and contradictions in the doctrine of the Trinity, as well as in those doctrines which concern human nature. The word *persona* is a legal term, denoting an individual as the subject of rights and duties. In modern philosophy personality is the attribute of the thinking subject, the ego who is supposed to be able to say, *Cogito, ergo sum.* But it cannot be too strongly emphasised that neither the word nor the Western idea of a "person" has any existence in

Greek, or in the theology of Greek-speaking Christians. I think I cannot illustrate this statement better than by quoting the following sentence from the treatise *De Persona et duabus Naturis,* falsely ascribed to Boëthius. The writer is defining, and finding Latin equivalents for, the Greek philosophical terms which express being. "Man," he says, "is οὐσία, quoniam est; he is οὐσίωσις (subsistentia) quoniam in nullo subjecto est (*i.e.* he has an independent existence, and is not a mere attribute or quality of something else); he is ὑπόστασις (substantia), quoniam subest ceteris qui substantise non sunt (*i.e.* he is the subject of qualities or attributes); and he is πρόσωπον (persona), quoniam est rationale individuum." Now *persona* may mean "rationale individuum," but irpovunrov means nothing of the kind. And the Latins soon saw that *tres personae* was very different from rpia TrpoacoTra, the latter expression being much more Sabellian in sound. Τρεῖς ὑποστάσεις, the accepted term, ought to mean three Substances, not three Persons. The result of this discrepancy, or rather of the dissimilar modes of thought reflected in the two languages, is that Western thought has generally been somewhat nearer to Tritheism and further from Modalism than Greek orthodoxy. Any approach to Tritheism makes St. John and the theology based upon him unintelligible; but unfortunately, with our notions of personality it is very difficult not to think of the Trinity as *tres personae* in the Latin sense, or even as three "Persons" in the modern sense, which is Tritheism pure and simple.

Medieval theology generally distinguished the Three Persons as Power, Wisdom, and Love, the Holy Ghost being the *copula* between the Father and the Son. It is instructive to notice that to each of the Three Persons is assigned all these attributes. It is unnecessary to quote passages attributing Wisdom and Love to the Father. And when Jesus Christ is proclaimed to exercise a threefold office, as King, Prophet, and Priest, have we not in this triad the same attributes of Power, Wisdom, and Love which theology teaches to be those of the Three Persons of the Trinity? The Holy Ghost in like manner is Power and Wisdom as well as Love. Thus the three attributes of the Three Persons - and may we not say further that Wisdom, Power, and Love have been the Divine attributes which the Greek Church, the Roman Church, and the Protestant bodies respectively have been most ready to grasp? - are all attributes of each Person, and it is quite inadmissible to set them over against each other, as is done in transactional theories of the Atonement.

That the doctrine of the Trinity has a psychological basis has been long recognised by theology. Gregory of Nyssa (*Orat. Cat.* 2) says, "As we know the Logos by analogy from our own nature, so in our own thoughts about the Spirit we may find a shadow and copy of His unspeakable power in our own nature." St. Augustine (*De Civ. Dei,* 11, 26) finds an image of the Trinity in the fact that "we are, and know ourselves to be, and love our being and knowing." He adds that these psychological states are more certain and immediate than any sensations from without. Alcuin, following the traditional classification of the faculties as intelligence, will, and memory, finds in them an image of the Trinity in Unity. "They are not three lives, but one life; not three minds, but one mind; not three substances, but one substance. For I understand that I understand, will, and remember: I will that I understand, remember, and will: and I remember that I understand, will, and remember" (*De An. Rat.,* 147). The mystics dwell much on this analogy. It is elaborated by Scotus Erigena, by Hylton in his *Scale of Perfection,* and by Julian of Norwich. Eckhart calls the Trinity "natured Nature" and the Unity "unnatured Nature." The distinction between the Divine Essence and the Persons, which he found in Thomas Aquinas, is fearlessly emphasised. The Godhead is above all relations, even above the relations of Father, Son, and Spirit.

The two points which I wish to emphasise about the doctrine of the Trinity are, first, that popular theology, when it thinks of the Three Persons in one God, is usually much more tritheistic than the orthodox faith. This error has come about through the unfortunate use of the word "Person," with its misleading associations. The other is that the analogy between the "Persons" of the Trinity and our own complex nature is not an accidental or fanciful resemblance, but rests on the belief that man is really a microcosm, reproducing in little the Creator in whose image he was made.

But my main subject to-day is the permanent value of the Logos-doctrine, the formula which converted the intellect of Europe to Christianity.

It is a significant fact that neither in German nor in English, nor (more important still) in Latin, is there any word which really represents the Greek term. Just as Goethe's Faust wavered between word, thought, and power, so the Latins debated whether *Verbum, Sermo,* or *Ratio* was the nearest equivalent of Logos in their language. Tertullian (Apol. 21) uses

Sermo and *Ratio* together to represent the single word Logos, as used by philosophers of the Agent in creation. They ultimately decided, as we know, on *Verbum* only, and we have followed them by choosing *Word;* but the Greek "Logos" has lost half its meaning in being thus translated, and the range of the ideas which it once conveyed has been narrowed and half forgotten. Indeed, the term is, except to theological students, so nearly meaningless that it has almost dropped out of the vocabulary of piety.

It would be possible to take up a great deal of time in discussing whether St. John got the expression from Philo or from some other source, and whether the Logos-doctrine is wholly Greek, or partly Jewish, in its origin. The affiliation of ideas is a difficult, and perhaps not a very fruitful subject of investigation. It is more important for us to know what St. John meant by calling Jesus Christ the Logos, than what were the sources from which he drew the conception.

It is characteristic of the Greeks, a nation of talkers, that the same word in their language should mean *speech* and *reason*. This comprehensiveness of the term certainly made it easier for Greek and Jewish philosophy to unite in dealing with the self-revelation of God in the creation and history of the world. For while the Greeks meant chiefly "Reason" by Logos, the Jews, when they spoke in Greek, meant chiefly "Word." There is no ambiguity about the Hebrew term "the Word of the Lord" in the Old Testament: it means the spoken word, not the thought, of Jehovah. If we collect the passages where "the Word of the Lord," and similar expressions occur in the Old Testament, we shall find that they are connected with three ideas those of creation, providence, and revelation. God "spoke the word" and the worlds were made: then at once His Spirit, the breath of His mouth, gives life to what His word creates and renews the face of the earth. The protecting care shown by God to the chosen people is attributed by all Jewish commentators to the Memra or Word, even where the sacred texts have the name Jehovah. And it is always the word of the Lord which inspires prophecy and imparts the Law. The tendency to personify the self-revealing activity of Jehovah becomes more and more marked. The angel of the Lord, the name, the presence, the glory of Jehovah, are frequently spoken of as if they were half personal beings, and later, the Divine Kochmah or Wisdom attains an almost complete hypostasis. The writer of Ecclesiasticus (i. 4) says that Wisdom was "created before all things," a doctrine which resembles the Arian Christology. The Wisdom of

Solomon goes still further in making Wisdom the cosmic principle. "Wisdom," says the writer, "is more moving than any motion. She passeth and goeth through all things by reason of her pureness. For she is the breath of the power of God, and a pure influence flowing from the glory of the Almighty. She is the brightness of the everlasting light, the unspotted mirror of the power of God, and the image of His goodness. She is one, but she can do all things; she remaineth in herself, but she maketh all things new; and in all ages entering into holy souls, she rnaketh them friends of God, and prophets. She reacheth from one end of the world to the other; and sweetly doth she order all things." But here we are no longer within the range of purely Jewish thought. The Wisdom literature has entered into the inheritance of Greek philosophy. To this *Greek* Logos-doctrine I now invite your attention for a few minutes.

The history of the Logos-idea begins with Heraclitus, that profoundly interesting Ephesian thinker whom his contemporaries nicknamed "the obscure," but whose scanty fragments contain flashes of the most penetrating brilliance. We cannot wonder that the Christian apologists of the second century coupled him with Socrates, as a man who "lived in accordance with the eternal reason" (Logos), and who might even be called a Christian before Christ, when we find in him such parallels to Christian teaching as the following: "This Logos existeth from all time, yet mankind are unaware of it, both before they hear it and while they listen to it." Compare St. John: "He was in the world, and the world knew Him not. He came unto His own, and His own received Him not." Or again, "The Logos is the judge of truth, that is, of the divine truth which is common to all" ("the true light which lighteth every man coming into the world"). "For that which environs us is rational and intelligent. We draw in the truth by inspiration." His Logos is the immanent reason and light of the world; its material emblem is fore. (Compare "again St. John Baptist's words about our Lord: "He shall baptize you with the Holy Ghost and with fire.") "The fire when it cometh shall try everything," he says, in words which suggest a well-known passage of St. Paul. The Logos, like Wordsworth's "Duty," keeps the sun and stars in their courses. In one aspect, it is the same as fate or destiny, or rather it is the rational principle which exhibits itself as unvarying law. It is the hidden harmony which underlies the perpetual strife, in which the life of the world as we know it subsists. It is the unifying principle of the world, and it is by participation in it that we come to ourselves. "To those who are awake," he says, "there is one common world, but sleepers have each a world of their own."

It is very significant that Heraclitus was scarcely dead before his disciples split into a right and left wing, precisely as did those of Hegel after his death. His philosophy was claimed on the one side as a vindication of conservative orthodoxy, on the other as sceptical and revolutionary. On the whole, the former view predominated. When the school of Heraclitus was absorbed into Stoicism, the Heracliteans in that school were the right wing, the orthodox and conservative branch, the Cynics the left wing. Modern students are by no means agreed what was the real tendency of his system; they quarrel about him exactly as they do about Hegel. Some label him a "pantheistic materialist." Even in his own day he was accused of making fire God. A more tenable charge is that his Logos was merely the rational self-evolution of the world, which was impersonal, and only attained to self-consciousness in man. Certainly Heraclitus seems to acknowledge no transcendent God, whose "Word" the Logos could be.

Plato's Logos-doctrine is to be found chiefly in the *Timaeus,* in which he teaches that the universe is produced by the "fusion of necessity and mind" ("mind," since Anaxagoras, had displaced Heraclitus' word Logos). The world is "a living and rational organism," the "only-begotten" (μονογενὴς) Son of God, itself a God, and the express image (εἰκὼν) of the Highest.

In the writings of the Stoics the word Logos again comes into prominence. Their "seminal Logos" is God Himself as the organic principle of the universe, directing it to a rational and moral end. They are often called Pantheists; but I think myself that this name should be reserved for those who hold that God is present *equally* in every part of His creation. We all believe in the omnipresence and immanence of the Deity, but we could not endorse the words of the Indian philosopher who said, "The learned behold God alike in the reverend Brahmin, in the ox and in the elephant, in the dog and in him who eateth the flesh of dogs," nor Pope's line that God is "As full, as perfect, in a hair as heart." The Stoics recognised an ascending scale of being: it was only to man that the Logos descended in such a way that his personality might be regarded as an actual portion of the Logos. This last notion led to the assurance that God is actually the guest of the human soul, constituting what is, or ought to be, the ruling and guiding principle of our lives. The Stoics also taught that we have communion with each other through our participation in the Logos, which remains *one* and the self-same spirit, though he divides to every man severally as he wills. It is to the Stoics, moreover, that we owe the distinction between the Logos ἐνδιάθετος and προφορικὸς - the former the unspoken thought, the inner psychical function, the latter the thought expressed in word and act. This distinction was the foundation of much Christian speculation on the relations between the Word and the Father. Stoical, too, is the recognition of the double meaning in Logos - not "thought" only, but "spoken word." I do not think there is any trace of this second conception before Plato, who comes near it once or twice, and Aristotle, who once distinguishes the "Word in the Soul" from the "outer Word"; but in Stoicism it is prominent. This made a bridge between Greek and Jewish ways of thinking, for with the Jews, as I have said, "the Word" meant the spoken utterance, not "thought." The Stoical notion was probably based on the belief that a spoken word is not merely a mode of expressing thought, but that it is a kind of spiritual form assumed by thought, having a real existence of its own. Belief in the living power of a spoken word is a common phase of superstition; it has, for instance, an important place in the Runic ritual of Northern Europe. In any case, this double connotation of the philosophical term Logos, which the uses of the word in ordinary speech made almost inevitable, had a very important influence on Alexandrian theology, in which the Greek and Jewish streams of thought flowed into each other.

Jewish philosophy could supply the most glaring defect of Stoicism - the belief in a transcendent God. The Stoic's God was really only Natural Law, and Plotinus, though not altogether unsympathetic towards them, could say, "They only bring in God, in order to be in the fashion." This is too severe; for it is a truly religious profession to say (and believe) that the laws of nature are the laws of God. But if we would avoid Pantheism, we must worship a God who is above as well as in the world, and this the Alexandrian *Philo,* who for us represents the complete fusion of Hellenic and Jewish thought, was careful to do. He describes God as unqualified and pure Being, to whom no names can be given. The Logos dwells with Him as His vicegerent. He is the "eldest son" of God, says Philo, mythically, and the "Wisdom of God" is His mother. In other places the Logos himself is called the Wisdom of God. Again, he is the Idea of Ideas, the whole mind of God when it goes out of itself in the act of creation. By His agency the worlds were made. He represents the world before God as High Priest, Intercessor, Paraclete. He is the Shechinah or glory of God; He is also the Darkness or Shadow of God, since the Creation half veils and half reveals the Deity. He is the intelligible world, the archetypal universe, of the Platonists, and the real life of the world that we know. He is in the closest relations with the human spirit, operating in man as the higher reason. And yet, with all these resemblances to the Johannine doctrine, Philo's Logos is not a hypostasis of the Deity. He is not personal, and may equally well be spoken of in the plural number. He is not so much the "Word" as the "Mind" of God. A true incarnation (as opposed to a theophany) of such a Being is unthinkable, and Philo never attempts to connect the Logos with the Messianic hopes of his people. Thus, whether or not St. John borrowed the terra Logos from Philo and his school, the cornerstone of the Johannine theology, the doctrine that "the Word became flesh," was not only not taken from Philo, but was totally opposed to his philosophy.

Such, then, were the antecedents of the term Logos, which the New Testament applies to Christ. It is of the doctrine in the New Testament that I now wish to speak. But before we come to the prologue of St. John's Gospel, I wish to show that St. Paul gives us a very complete and explicit Logos-theology, though he never uses the word. I wish to lay special stress on this point, because none of the commentators on St. Paul, so far as I know, do full justice to it. I am convinced that the conception of Christ as a cosmic principle - that conception which is enunciated in St. John's prologue - holds a *more* important place in St. Paul's theology than in that of St. John, and that it may be proved, not only from his later Epistles, which some critics, partly on this account, consider spurious, but from those which are not disputed. I will collect the chief passages which, taken together, comprise St. Paul's teaching on this subject, naming in each case the Epistle from which the words are taken.

In relation to God the Father, Christ is the Image (εἰκὼν) of God (2 Cor., Col.). This is a Philonic term, with a well-defined connotation. An εἰκὼν is a copy, not only resembling but derived from its prototype. It *represents* its prototype, and is a *visible manifestation* of it: Christ is the "εἰκὼν of the Invisible God" (Col.). In Him dwells bodily (σωματικῶς) the Pleroma, the totality of the Divine attributes (Col, Eph.). The special force of this phrase is that He needs no subordinate "thrones, dominions, or powers" to mediate between Him and the world. Philo's Logos was polarised, as it were, into various Logoi or δυνάμεις; in Christ there is no such delegation of energy. He is "Lord of all" and "Lord of Glory" (Rom., i Cor.); even (probably) "God over all, blessed for ever" (Rom. ix. 5.).

In reference to the world, Christ is the Agent in creation; "through Him are all things" (i Cor. viii. 6), and we through Him. He pre-existed "in the form of God" (Phil. ii. 6) from the beginning. He is "the first-born of all creation; in Him and through Him and unto Him are all things. He is before all things, and in Him all things hold together" (Col. i. 15, 16). All things are to be summed up in Him (Eph. i. 10). "He is *all* and in all" (Col. iii. 11). His reign is co-extensive with the world's history. "He must reign till He hath put all His enemies under His feet. The last enemy that shall be abolished is death." Only "when all things have been subjected unto Him, shall the Son also Himself be subjected to Him that did subject all things unto Him, that God may be all in all" (i Cor. xv. 24-28).

In reference to the human soul, "The Lord is the Spirit" (2 Cor. iii. 17); He is "life-giving Spirit" (i Cor. xv. 45). As such He is the possession of all true Christians, "living in them" (Gal. ii. 20); "forming Himself in them" (Gal. iv. 19); "transforming them into His image" (2 Cor. iii. 18); enlightening their understandings, so that they can judge all things, even searching out "the hidden things of God" (i Cor. iii. 15), and uniting them in closest union with each other and with Himself.

These quotations, which might easily be multiplied, seem to me to contain all the elements of a complete Logos-theology; and it is a constant source of surprise to me that critics continue to say that the Pauline Christ is only "the heavenly man," and that for a complete recognition of Christ as the Logos we must wait for the fourth Gospel. It is of no avail to deny the authenticity of the Epistles to the Colossians and Ephesians, for some of the most striking declarations come, as I have shown, from the undisputed Epistles. For my own part, though the style and phraseology of the later Epistles differ slightly from the earlier, I cannot trace any development or modification of doctrine, except that the pronouncements on eschatology become more spiritual, and less affected by chiliastic beliefs, as we advance from 1 Thessalonians to Colossians. But this is just what we should have expected: the hopes of a future earthly "reign of the saints" were deeply rooted in Judaism and Judaic Christianity; they were undermined by the Logos-theology, which, as we can see, gradually overcame them in St. Paul's own mind.

The Pauline Logos-doctrine is, to me, so supremely important that I should like to sum up again the chief heads of it, especially as regards the second of the three divisions, the relation of Christ to the world. I choose this part for special emphasis, not because it is tho most important, but because it is, unfortunately, as I venture to think, almost entirely neglected in modern religious teaching.

St. Paul does not speculate at all on the relations of the Son to the Father apart from creation. The words "He was before all things" are sufficient to exclude the Arian dogma, ἦν ὅτε οὐκ ἦν, whatever interpretation we give to the πρωτότοκος πάσης κτίσεως of Colossians. So far as we can know, the reign of the Son as a distinct principle in the Godhead is co-extensive with time; it began "in the beginning," and will continue till "cometh the end." For us, the Son is the revelation of God in space and time. I do not think we shall get any profit by speculating on His relations to the Father *outside* those categories; the recognition of His unity with the Father is enough to guard us against the notion that He has *only* a temporal life. The Son, then, is the creating and sustaining principle in the universe: He comprehends it, though as God He is not comprehended by it. All the life in the world is His life; the fulfilment of His will is the far-off divine event to which the whole creation moves. He was in the world from the first, though the world knew Him not; He was the spiritual rock that followed the Israelites; He was the "mystery" which shrouded all the higher aspirations of those who lived under the old dispensation, till in the fulness of time it was revealed in the historical Christ.

It may be asked why St. Paul avoids the word Logos, while he gives us, in his doctrine of Christ, all that the word contains? I have no answer to suggest; for it is nearly certain that the word had found a home in Jewish theology some time before Philo. We must be content to note the fact without explaining it; and we may now pass to the prologue of the fourth Gospel, where the Divinity and Incarnation of the Logos are explicitly asserted.

The doctrine of the prologue is, so far as I can see, identical with that of St. Paul. The Word, as God in essence, has an extra-temporal relation in closest union with the Father. He is the agent and the quickening spirit in creation, the life of all that lives, and the light of all that shines. That light had brooded over all history, enlightening every man, but unrecognised by many. At last came the time when "the Logos became flesh and tabernacled among us, and we beheld His glory, the glory as of the only-born Son of the Father, full of grace and truth."

I think, then, that we may say that the Logos-doctrine of the prologue is identical with that of St. Paul. And yet we all feel that, even apart from differences of style, it would be impossible to attribute any page of St. John to St. Paul, or vice versa. What is the main difference between them?

We are so familiar with St. Paul's Epistles as part of the New Testament that we have probably seldom thought about what is surely a very strange and remarkable feature in them - the extreme paucity of references to the human life of Christ: to His pithy, illuminating sayings, which fix themselves so firmly in the memory, and lend themselves so readily to quotation; to His parables; to His works of healing, and so on. We should have expected *a priori* that such a number of didactic and hortatory epistles on the religion of Christ, written within a few years of His death, would have supplied us with almost enough material for a fifth Gospel. Instead of that, there is hardly a word, hardly an incident, for which the biographer of Christ can appeal to St. Paul. He seems determined to know nothing of Jesus but the bare facts of the crucifixion and resurrection. In one place he says that he wishes to know no man, not even Christ, any more after the flesh. I do not wish to lay undue stress on this last passage, for I believe "to know no longer after the flesh" means mainly to know as an immortal spirit, to view personality *sub specie aeternitatis;* but surely, when we consider the circumstances of St. Paul's conversion, it is very significant that he did not trouble himself to collect all the information he could procure about the earthly life and teaching of His Master. If he had done so, if he had learnt by heart or transcribed for his own use even as much of our Lord's discourses as have survived in the synoptic Gospels, we *must* have had frequent quotations and references to them in his Epistles. As such quotations and references are conspicuously absent, we are driven to the conclusion that St. Paul was content with the most general information as to the main heads of our Lord's teaching and the impression which His character made on those who had known Him, and that he preferred to rest his own religion and theology entirely on the inner light vouchsafed to him, and on the bare facts of the death and resurrection of the Son of God. And what especially interested him about the death and resurrection was the light which they throw on the spiritual life of human beings. The life and death and rising again of Christ are to him a kind of dramatisation of the normal psychological experience. We, too, must die to sin and rise again to righteousness; nay, we must die daily, crucifying the old man and putting on the new man - the true likeness of Him who created us. And this is why the identification of Christ with the world-principle was so essential for him. The "whole process of Christ" (as some of our English divines called it) was thus proved to be the great spiritual law under which we all live. Whatever it behooved Christ to do and to suffer, that we, as members of His body, must be prepared to do and suffer also. If God was pleased highly to exalt Him who in human form did and suffered such things, then for us too death has lost its sting and the grave its victory. The law of the universe is proved to be not the law of sin and death, but the law of redemption through suffering, ending in triumph over sin and death. This I believe is the leading thought in St. Paul's theology; and it is easy to see that it is in no way dependent on any historical details about the human Christ. Having once accepted the "revelation" made to him about the Person of Christ, he was, we may say boldly, independent of the history.

When we turn to St. John, we find a great difference St. John chose to make his main work a Gospel, not an epistle or a series of epistles. And in his first Epistle he insists with the strongest emphasis on the historical facts which he has himself seen and heard, and on the decisive importance of "confessing that Jesus Christ has come in the flesh." Indeed, except in the prologue, the cosmological side of the Logos-doctrine falls very much into the background. It is assumed, but not insisted on, as it is by St. Paul. The relation of the Word to the universe generally does not occupy St. John's thoughts; his mind is less philosophical than St. Paul's. The two men lay hold of the Gospel message from different sides. Instead of "Christ who died, nay rather, who is risen again," the central doctrine for St. John is "the Word was made flesh and tabernacled among us, and we beheld His glory." St. Paul thinks more of redemption, St. John of revelation. St. Paul loves to dwell on the crucifixion, St. John on the incarnation. Both alike lay the greatest possible stress on the mystical union between the risen Christ and His members, and (which is the same thing) the inspiring, illuminating, and sanctifying presence of the Holy Ghost in the Church; but St. John includes in his teaching, and regards as an essential part of it, a clear and definite presentation of the life and work of Christ on earth. According to him, the office of the Spirit is not to act in us as an independent and infallible source of spiritual knowledge, but to bring to our remembrance the teachings of Christ which we read in the Gospels. No doubt our Lord promises that the Spirit of truth shall guide the Church into all truth, including some things which the earliest disciples "could not bear" to hear, but the historical records remain as a check and test; those who follow St. John cannot allow themselves quite so much liberty as some expressions in St. Paul seem to sanction.

The fourth Gospel is frankly and avowedly written with a purpose. Its materials are selected and arranged with a definite object, which is stated at the conclusion of chapter xx., where the Gospel really ends - chapter xxi. is merely an appendix. St. John's object is to make his' readers believe that the man Jesus is (1) the Messiah, (2) the Son of God or the Logos (as those terms were understood by religious thinkers at that time), and "that believing they might have life through His name."

His treatment of history is very characteristic. He combines Philo's allegorism with the positivism which is more natural to Jewish thought. He would accept Goethe's dictum that "all that is transitory is only a symbol," with the exception of the word *only*. In his hands every event is a type, a symbol, an illustration of some aspect of the nature and character of the Divine Logos. Our Lord's miracles are all acted parables, and the evangelist generally gives us the key to their interpretation, *e.g.* "I am the Bread of Life," "I am the Light of the World." Even accidental coincidences have a meaning for him, as when Judas turns away from the supper-table and goes out to his doom "and it was night"; or when Caiaphas spoke more truly than he knew, and said, "It is expedient that one man should die for the people." Every incident in the Gospel is selected for its symbolical value; the events, miracles, and discourses are so arranged as to exhibit in a series of pictures the various aspects of the Incarnate Word. But even when so treated, St. John does not wish us to make the outward history the basis of our faith. The various "works" which our Lord did, as parts of His one "work," the "work" which the Father "gave Him to do" (xvii. 4), whether natural or supernatural (it is needless to say that there is no trace of this unfortunate classification in St. John), are a "witness" to Him (v. 36, xiv. 11), a witness "greater" than that of John the Baptist (v. 36); but they are a lower kind of witness than His words. The Johannine Christ puts the words above the works. He tells Philip that "he that believeth on Him shall do even greater works than these," but He does not say, and could not say, "greater words than these shall he speak." And in the sixth chapter, when both "Jews" and "disciples" show such a strange inability to grasp the symbolic meaning of the "bread which came down from heaven," our Lord closes the discussion by saying, "It is the spirit that quickeneth, the flesh profiteth nothing. The *words* that *I* have spoken" (the pronoun is emphatic and the verb is in the perfect tense) - the words that I have spoken, not the miracle that I have wrought - "they are spirit and they are life." And in the twentieth chapter, who can fail to see that the climax even of the resurrection story and the conclusion of the whole narrative of our Lord's ministry is to be sought in that most impressive sentence, the last words of our Lord in the Gospel proper, "Blessed are they that have not seen and yet have believed." It is impossible to exaggerate the importance of these words, coming where they do, at the end of a great historical narrative, and in closest connection with the evidence for the resurrection. St. John, the historian of our Lord's death and resurrection, deliberately records and gives the supreme place of honour to the beatitude which our Lord refused to the man who demanded evidence of a miracle, and bestowed on those who believe without such evidence. For this and nothing else is the meaning of the whole story, as every candid reader must admit. And it is, I believe, one of the most precious lessons of the fourth Gospel. I shall not be suspected of holding a brief for those who believe "because they choose," or because "doubt is a sin." But I see in this deliberate placing of our Lord's *words* above His works a recognition of a truth which some of us are, from the best of motives, too reluctant to admit. I mean, that a purely historical faith appeals only to the *understanding,* to the faculty which judges of scientific or historical truth in other fields; that the conclusions it arrives at are as liable to be upset as the conclusions of secular historians; and that it is subject to the limitations which Bacon asserts of intellectual investigations generally - "Studies teach not their own use." The *words* of Christ appeal not to the senses and understanding, but to the heart and higher reason. They sound in our ears as coming from another, but they are echoed within us by that "Witness" of which St. John speaks in his Epistle - that still small voice which is nothing else than the voice of the Paraclete who dwells within us for this very purpose. "The words which I speak unto you, they are spirit and they are life." They never lose their freshness; they are exempt from change and decay; though heaven and earth pass, they shall not fail; they are the living thoughts of the ever-living and never-changing Logos, thoughts of which all things that happen on this planet are but illustrations and examples.

The historical facts are important - no one feels this more strongly than St. John: they are important because they once happened, and everything that has happened lives for ever in the mind of God. But their importance does not lie in the fact that they happened only once. That is a strange notion which many people seem to cherish about the Gospel history, and it makes them terribly distressed when any attacks are made upon what they call the foundations of their faith. St. John sees in Christ the Light that lighteth *every* man, to know whom is eternal life. He thus allows the experience of the Christian Church to throw light upon the Gospel history, instead of making the historical records bear the whole weight of the Church's faith. "These things are written," he says, "that ye may believe that Jesus is the Christ, the Son of God." St. John never calls the body of his teaching a knowledge, a γνῶσις. Fond as he is of the verb to know, he studiously avoids the substantive, just as he avoids the substantive "faith" (πίστις) while frequently using the verb "to believe." These are not insignificant facts; they are all part of St. John's religious philosophy. The Gospel narrative is to be studied "*in order that we may know*": it does not convey knowledge immediately. "Getting to know" is a gradual process, a progressive inner experience. God reveals Himself within us as we are able to receive Him, and at each stage the figure of the historical Christ becomes clearer and more intelligible to us. In this way the faith that began as an experiment ends as an experience; the body of teaching which we at first received from outside becomes part of our very selves. "If any man willeth to do His will, he shall know of the doctrine," is the promise. Let us once and for all have done with the apprehension that that which shines and burns among us as the very life of our life, closer to us than breathing, and nearer than hands and feet, can ever be "disproved," "refuted," or filched from us in any way, by the digging up of an old scrap of papyrus, or the ingenious lucubrations of some German professor. The history of the world is for St. John the history of a living and growing organism. What the Logos is, that He was two thousand years ago. What He is, we may in some sort hope to know even better than those who then heard Him, for the Spirit of Truth cannot have been teaching mankind for two thousand years entirely in vain. And the way to know Him as He is is always the same, to keep His commandments.

I have expatiated on the Johannine view of history, and its relation to universal and eternal truth, because I have found it myself the most steadying and reassuring doctrine in this age of doubt. It sets us free from that haunting fear - which is surely an unworthy and faithless fear - that the honest exercise of the highest intellectual faculties, whether in scholarship, criticism, or the study of nature's laws, may lead to the discovery of something that had better not have been discovered. St. John has no fears that his portrait of Jesus Christ will ever fade or be convicted of untruthfulness. He appeals with absolute confidence to the "witness" which every man's heart will bear, to the end of time, to his veracity. The Spirit of Truth will never leave the human race, and will always tell them the same tale. "Let that, therefore, abide in you which ye have heard from the beginning. The anointing which ye have received of Him abideth in you, and ye need not that any man teach you; but as the same anointing teacheth you of all things, and is truth, and is no lie, and even as it has taught you, ye shall abide in Him." I ask you to consider the sublime confidence in the unity and rationality of the world's life, which this attitude of the evangelist towards posterity displays. He tells us a wonderful story, and asks all future ages to believe it on his testimony. And he has no doubt that they will believe it. Why? Simply because it is the truth, and what has happened once is and must be part of the law of the universe, which verifies itself afresh in each generation. Never once does he corroborate his narrative by "witnesses" in his own generation: the witnesses on whom he relies are his readers themselves, most of them yet unborn, and the never-silent voice of the Spirit of Truth in their hearts. I know of no more splendid instance of the faith that *magna est veritas, et praevalebit.*

[1] 2 Cor. iii. 17.

Three - Development and Permanent Value of the Logoschristology

It is not part of my plan in these lectures to deal historically with the old Christological controversies; but since the questions which divide theologians to-day are at bottom very much the same as those which agitated the Church in the second, third, and fourth centuries, it may be convenient to take two or three of these early divisions as examples of permanent tendencies. We find almost from the first a school of theology which had no room for speculations about the Logos - I mean the Adoptian theology. To this school belonged the so-called "Alogi" of the second century, who ascribed the Johannine writings to Cerinthus, and rejected the whole Logos-theology, claiming, like their modern successors, to "return to the historical Christ," whose portrait they found, again like their modern successors, in St. Mark. They hated "prophesyings" of the Puritan or Montanist kind, and eschewed emotional mystical religion. The Roman Adoptians were exegetical scholars and Aristotelians, like the Ritschlians to-day: the Antiochene school took up their work and their principles half a century later. Paul of Samosata was a vigorous representative of this type. He wished to get rid of metaphysics and Platonism, and taught that the uniqueness of Christ was in His character, not in His nature. Then came Arianism, which was a compromise between the Logos-doctrine and the Adoptian theology. It would have led Christianity back towards both Judaism and Paganism. Towards Paganism, in so far as it deifies a creature and abolishes the unity of God; towards Judaism, as it makes the union of God and man impossible, by the interpolation of a third being who is neither God nor man. All competent theologians now agree that Arianism was one of the most illogical and contradictory of heresies, and that Athanasius was absolutely justified in refusing any of the plausible compromises that were offered to him.

But the most vigorous though not the most irreconcilable opponent of the Logos-Christology from 180-300 was *Modalism.* This controversy was singularly like that which had raged between Stoicism and Platonism, the Medalists or Monarchians being the representatives of the Stoics. In fact these Church controversies were the old philosophical battles fought out again with new weapons. As the Adoptianists were Aristotelian, so the Modalists were Stoic, and (to use a later word) *nominalist.* They taught that such designations as Father and Son are merely accidental attributes, so that the same subject can in one relation be Father, in another Son, in one relation visible, in another invisible. On the other hand, orthodox Catholicism, or rather that which after its victory was recognised as such, was Platonic. Even to this day, I doubt whether any one can be an orthodox theologian without being a Platonist. Our creeds are the formulae of victorious Platonism. The Monarchians or Modalists, however, were not wholly in the wrong as against the Platonists. The Logos of Alexandrian Platonism was not "equal to the Father" even as touching his Godhead. The mere fact of His being *derived,* and not the fountain-head of Godhead, proved him (according to this school) to be inferior. And so we find that even Alexandrian orthodoxy was half-subordinationist in the third century. The Sabellians were more orthodox in maintaining the identity, and therefore the equality, of the revealed God with the Father. In the fourth century, however, the Arian danger drove orthodoxy into something like a compromise with Modalism. The test-word ὁμοούσιος gave the Monarchians most of what they wanted, and its adoption soon ended the hostility of this school.

But we must consider a little more closely the attitude of Athanasius, the dominant spirit of the anti-Arian controversy, towards the Alexandrian Platonism which remains the classical example of a Christianity based on the Logos-doctrine. Harnack is strongly convinced that the Athanasian theology virtually discards the Logos, as understood by Clement and Origen. "The Logos of the philosophers was no longer the Logos whom he (Athanasius) knew and adored." By this he means that in Athanasius the close connection of the second Person of the Trinity with the life of the universe is dissolved. Nature and Revelation are no longer regarded as different aspects of the same thing. The Logos is no longer a world-principle, but a salvation-principle. The Divine in Christ is for him no longer the world-reason, the world -spirit.

These statements raise very difficult questions. The Logos-doctrine of Clement and Origen is none too clear. These Christian thinkers found ready to their hand the Stoic distinction between the Logos ἐνδιάθετος and the Logos προφορικός: they tended to accept this distinction, and to speak almost as if there was one Logos of the Father (impersonal) and another of the Son. Both Clement and Origen, especially the former, were accused of making *two* Logoi. This seems to have been actually the view of some Gnostic sects, for in the apocryphal Acts of John, Jesus is represented as saying, "Glory to Thee, Father, glory to Thee, Logos, glory to Thee, Holy Spirit," and in the apocryphal Gospel of Peter, the dying Christ cries, "My Power, my Power, thou hast forsaken me," the "Power" being the heavenly Christ, who for a time had been associated with the earthly person of the Redeemer. The difficulty was to reconcile the doctrine of the *unchangeableness* of God, to which they attached great importance, with the changes and contingencies of terrestrial life. The Alexandrians were deeply imbued with the Platonic or idealistic belief that everything that *happens* is the outer manifestation of a timeless, supramundane truth. From this point of view, historical events, however sublime, are but *illustrations,* not *causes,* of eternal facts. This leads Clement and Origen to take a rather independent and high-handed line with regard to Scripture history. They considered that what is important in history is not the facts themselves, but the universal truths which they illustrate or symbolise. So Origen speaks of the actions of Christ during his ministry as αἰνίγματα - acted parables. Athanasius felt more strongly than the Alexandrians the importance of the *redemptive* side of Christ's work; this part of Christian teaching receives quite a new emphasis in his writings. And also, which is more to the point for our present subject, he is determined that the Son of God, the Logos, shall not be *identified* with the world-idea. He insists (to use modern language) that the Son as well as the Father is transcendent and not merely immanent. This leads him to the very verge of Sabellian-ism; for while he calls the Son ὁμοούσιος τῷ πατρὶ, he repeatedly identi-fies οὐσία with ὑπόστασις, and ὑπόστασις is, as we have seen, the ac-cepted Greek word for person. In one passage only he takes fright, and says that ὁμοούσιος is not the same as μονοούσιος," as the Sabellians think," but he does not explain the difference. And yet I believe we may say that this part of Athanasius' teaching not only does not overthrow or discard the Logos-doctrine, but that it is of the highest value as rescuing it from the danger of Pantheism.

Those Christian philosophers who had identified the Logos with the Neoplatonic Noi/9 could not indeed be accused of disparaging the Son, for they left nothing above him but the First Person of the Neoplatonic Trinity, the super-essential, superpersonal One, the Absolute. But the great religious danger was that this unapproachable God might be hidden in His own darkness, and that the Logos Christ, only accidentally, as it were, connected with the man Christ Jesus, might no longer bring men into communion with Him. The Neoplatonists indeed had their κόσμος νοητὸς - their ideal world, the sphere of the thoughts of God, and there-fore of the highest reality, between "the One" and the self-evolving World-Spirit; but Christian theology tended to identify the Νοῦς with the Logos, and had no equivalent for the Neoplatonic third Person, the "Soul" or World -Spirit. The Arian created Logos was nearly in the place of this third principle, and he was in no essential connection with the Father. The Athanasian doctrine, which became fixed as the orthodox one, safeguards the transcendence and the immanence of the God who made the world, and in so doing returns more completely to the doctrine of the fourth Gospel than had any earlier scheme. I cannot agree with Harnack that the ὁμοούσιος doctrine is a tissue of absurdities and contradictions, any more than I can agree that it sacrifices the Logos-doctrine. It was only to be expected that the life-and-death struggle with Arianism should drive orthodoxy, for the time, a little too far in the direction of Modalism; but it was quite possible to give Athanasianism a consistent basis, as indeed was shown very soon after. The Logos, in relation to the Father, is the totality of His mind and will; in relation to the world He is the Power that made it and sustains it in being, the Intelligence that guides it, and the Will that directs its life to a purposed end. The laws of the universe are God's laws, but neither God the Father nor the Logos is so bound up in them that it could be said that His life grows and accomplishes itself in the life of the world. This seems to be the main distinction between the Johannine and Athanasian Logos-doctrine on the one side and the modern idealistic philosophy of the school of Hegel, which in many ways so much resembles it, on the other. It is true that the cosmological aspect falls into the background both in St. John and in Athanasius; but that is because they are primarily religious teachers, not philosophers. The recognition of the Divine working everywhere, which makes Clement such a happy and optimistic theologian, is assuredly not forgotten.

Before leaving this side of our subject, I must just add that all theologians who worship Christ as the Logos have insisted that the generation of the Son by the Father is a continuous process, not a single act in the remotest past. "He was not begotten once for all; he is always being begotten," says Origen. Victorinus, the first *Latin* Christian Platonist, whose importance as an Augustinian before Augustine was first shown by Bishop Gore, speaks of the *semper generans generatio*; and this doctrine is repeated by the mystics, who like also to speak of Christ being "born in us," or "begotten in us" by the Father. Those who think thus, naturally hold that the Incarnation was not the consequence of man's fall, but was part of the eternal counsel of God, the chief object indeed of creation. This view r which Harnack says is the root of the Logos-doctrine, and which in the same breath he condemns as a "fantastic pantheism," is advocated by Clement, Theodore of Mopsuestia, and others, and has been defended in our days by Bishop Westcott, whose theology is thoroughly dominated by the Logos-doctrine. There is a great numerical preponderance in favour of the other view, that the fall of man was a *felix culpa* as making the Incarnation necessary; but I cannot help feeling that the former is the more beautiful and the more philosophical belief that the taking of the manhood into God was from the first the intention with which the human race was created, and that it occurred in history at the earliest possible moment.

I now come to the relation of the Logos-doctrine to personal religion. I will start by expressing my agreement with what has been said by Mr. Upton at the beginning of his Hibbert lectures, that "all wholly satisfying and effective religious belief arises out of the immediate feeling of God's self-revealing presence in our consciousness." "God lends a portion of His eternal life to us, that we may at length make it our own."

The Platonic, and still more the Stoic, speculation had led to the recognition of something divine in the spirit of man. In the more pantheistic Stoical form the doctrine might be expressed as follows: "The Godhead can unfold His essence in a variety of existences, which, while they are His creatures as to their origin, are parts of His essence as to their contents." This is not expressed in religious language; but the belief that the Spirit of God is actually the guest and guide of the human soul was the source of all that was best and most ennobling in the system of the Stoics.

Philo divides humanity into "heavenly" and "earthly" persons. "There are two classes of men," he says; "ὁ μὲν οὐράνιος ἄνθρωπος ὁ δὲ γήϊος. The heavenly man has no share in corruptible and earthly being." "That force which we share with irrational beings has for its οὐσία blood." This phraseology must have influenced St. John when he wrote "which were born not of blood, nor of the will of the flesh, nor of the will of man, but of God," and St. Peter when he wrote "born again, not of corruptible seed but of incorruptible"; and, most remarkable of all, the words in i John "the seed (of God) remaineth in him, and he cannot sin, because he is born of God." St. John clearly holds that the elect are in a very literal though spiritual sense sons of God. He says nothing about the relation of this sonship to that of Christ, and I think it is safer not to speculate about it. But do not let us put aside the passages that I have quoted as "mere metaphors."

The first Christian writer to develop the idea of the indwelling Logos is Justin. He borrows from the Stoics the expression σπέρμα τοῦ λόγου, "seed of the Logos," and teaches that all mankind have this "seed" as a natural possession. The best of the heathens, like Heraclitus and Socrates, might be called Christians before Christ. But knowledge, even when it comes from the σπέρμα τοῦ λόγου, seems merely human wisdom compared with the fulness and certainty of the knowledge imparted by the Logos-Christ.

The second century Apologists argue against the natural immortality of the human soul. Their doctrine is that immortality is conferred by the indwelling Logos. But immortality is the distinctive prerogative of the Divine nature, according to all Greek ideas; and the Logos cannot confer a greater privilege than He has Himself. So we get three dogmas, closely interconnected: *the Logos is God; redemption consists in the bestowal of immortality; and immortality is participation in the Divine nature.* I do not think it is too much to say that the two latter doctrines, now seldom preached in their original form, that salvation consists of union with God, and that exemption from the common lot of mortality is bound up with that union, were the weapons which finally struck down Arianism and similar heresies, and established the dogma of the full divinity of Christ. This opinion is very clearly stated by Harnack: "If actual interference in the constitution of human nature, and its deification, are involved, then the Redeemer must himself be God and must become man. With the satisfaction of these two conditions, real, natural redemption, that is to say, the deification of humanity, is actually effected. These considerations explain why Athanasius strove for the formula that the Logos-Christ was of the same nature as the Father, as though the existence or non-existence of the Christian religion were at stake. They show clearly how it was that other teachers in the Greek Church regarded any menace to the complete *unity* of the divine and human in the Redeemer, any notion of a merely moral connection, as a deathblow to Christianity." I think this is true, with the exception of the word "interference"; but I, of course, do not agree with what follows in Harnack's lecture, that the two doctrines with which (as he truly says) the Logos-doctrine stands or falls, are untenable. The former doctrine, which Harnack calls "deification," is simply the Pauline and Johannine mysticism, which no doubt has intoxicated many weak heads, but which, as St. Paul himself shows, may be the source of the very deepest humility and holy fear; while the notion of eternal life as the gift of God is only mischievous if it leads (as it did with some of the Greeks) to what I can only call a pharmacological superstition about the sacraments, as if the consecrated elements literally introduced an incorruptible substance into our bodies.

The Alexandrians, Clement and Origen, did not develop the idea of the immanent Logos beyond what we find in the Apologists. This was left to their opponent Methodius, who, though a Platonist, was not an Origenist. Methodius clearly believes the imperfection of the first Adam to have been natural, and sees in the Incarnation the necessary complement of the creation. The following extract will show how he combined a doctrine of development with the belief that the "whole process of Christ" must be enacted in the soul of every Christian: "The Church increases daily in greatness and beauty, because the Logos dwells with her and holds communion with her; and He even now descends to us, and in remembrance of His suffering dies continually to himself. For not otherwise could the Church continually receive believers in her womb, and bear them anew, unless Christ were continually to die, emptying Himself for the sake of each individual...No one can participate in the Holy Spirit unless the Logos has first descended upon him, and emptied Himself for him."

Augustine takes up the same idea. "If God were to cease from *speaking* the Word, even for a moment, heaven and earth would vanish." God is to him the ideal and presupposition of what he finds in his own soul. In the soul he finds the image of the Trinity, for we are, we know our being, and we love this being and knowing. (This last idea, that the Holy Ghost is the copula, who "in perfect love dost join the Father and the Son," is not, as is usually supposed, an original speculation of Augustine's, but is found in Victorinus, to whom he owes so much.) Of course he holds that this knowledge of God in the soul can only be imparted by God dwelling in the soul; for, like all Platonists, it is an axiom with him that only like can know like. Macarius, following Methodius, teaches that the very idea of the Incarnation includes the union of the Logos with pious souls, in whom He is well pleased. In each of them a Christ is born. Thus beside the ideas of Ransom and Sacrifice, of Christ *for* us, these theologians placed the ideas of sanctification and inner transformation, of Christ in us, and they considered the latter as real and as integral a part of our redemption as the former.

But the doctrine of Divine immanence in the human heart never became quite the central truth of theology till the time of the mediaeval mystics. It is Eckhart who says: "The Father speaks the Word into the soul, and when the Son is born, every soul becomes Mary." The deepest thoughts of Eckhart range round such texts as Rom. viii. 16, "The Spirit itself beareth witness with our spirit, that we are the children of God, and if children then heirs, heirs of God and join theirs with Christ"; or John xvii. 22, "The glory which Thou gavest Me I have given them, that they may be one even as We are one; I in them and Thou in Me, that they may be made perfect in one." The "*spark*" at the centre of the soul is the very presence of the divine Logos himself. Jerome is, I think, the first to use the queer word *synteresis* for this highest faculty of the soul. The whole object of our life here is to make this "spark" extend its light over the whole man, expelling and destroying that selfishness and isolation which is the principle of our false "self." Not only to die daily, but to be born daily, was the prayer of these saints. Eckhart the younger, having been 'asked what he deemed the highest of his spiritual experiences, replied, "Not the feeling, experience, tasting of God did he deem the highest that had happened to him, but that he should have overcome all the rebellion and disorder of his nature, that he should enjoy everywhere the presence of the divine light, that he should do everything in this light, and begin daily afresh, and be daily as a new-born child." The elder Eckhart has the following striking sentence: "God is nigh unto us, but we are far from Him; God is within, we are without; God is at home, we are strangers; God is always ready, we are very unready." Hugo of St. Victor sums up the whole creed of psychological mysticism when he says: "To ascend to God is to enter into oneself and to transcend oneself," and Richard expresses the same idea by "Ascendat per semetipsum supra semetipsum."

I cannot now give any further account of the manner in which the mediaeval mystics worked out the thought that Christ Himself, through the Holy Spirit, is the life of our life, the core of our being, who, if we could but rid ourselves entirely of our false self-regarding self, would be the constitutive force of our personality. What I wish to emphasise is that this doctrine, in which so many of God's saints have found blessedness, is the form of personal religion which belongs to the Logos-doctrine. I need not remind you that it is the foundation of St. Paul's Christianity, and the source of his strongest and most moving appeals. "I live, yet not I but

Christ liveth in me"; "to me to live is Christ" - these are revelations of the deepest experience, the strongest conviction, which animated that Apostle in his life of labour and suffering. The life, death, and resurrection of the Word of God were not a solitary event, not an unique portent, but the supreme vindication of an universal law. It is exemplified and re-enacted in little, in every human soul among the elect; it is in the highest sense of the word *natural,* for to those who can understand Scotus Erigena's words: "Be assured that the Word is the nature of all things," nothing is "supernatural." The best that God can give us, the gift of His own presence, is all part of His original scheme, part of the inviolable laws under which we live.

The "natural religion" which is based on belief in Divine immanence is very different from the lifeless, spectral creed which bore this name in the eighteenth century. It does not essay the hopeless task of "proving" the existence of God by the categories of the understanding; still less does it find a sorry satisfaction in confirming apparent injustices in revealed religion by parallel injustices in the course of nature. It is not pantheistic, but it does value and assert what Krause called *panentheism;* and in many thinkers, who are by no means fanciful dreamers, it produces a sympathy with what is known as *panpsychism,* the theory that nature is alive and even participant in soul-life throughout, though in very different degrees. This theory has been developed in a very interesting manner by Fechner, the great psychologist and philosopher.

It will be seen that the view of the Second Person of the Trinity which I have been taking - that which is based on St. John and St, Paul, and which has been developed by the Christian Platonists and speculative mystics - is above all things alien to the Ritschlian view that the impression of Christ which we derive from the synoptic Gospels is alone of religious value. It may no doubt be retorted upon me that the Logos-doctrine is really independent of the historical Incarnation; that it is a cosmological theory, a philosophy, not a religion. The whole Gospel history (it may be said) is on this theory merely propaedeutic or exoteric, milk for babes, as compared with the higher doctrine that the Word of God is incarnate in every believer. It is notorious that some of the Alexandrians did use language which gave a handle for this charge. Henry More, himself a mystic and Platonist, brings the same accusation against the Quakers. He taxes them with "slighting the history of Christ, and making a mere allegory of it, tending to the overthrow of that warrantable though more external frame of Christianity, which Scripture itself points out to us." [1] To make an "allegory" of events, whether in our own lives or in history, is undoubtedly a tendency with Platonists. What Origen calls "spiritual" as opposed to "somatic" Christianity, does tend to regard all real history as supramundane, the series of events which we call history being what is now called an epiphenomenon only. But we must distinguish. If we choose to say with Goethe that everything which is transitory is only a symbol of what is permanent, and to include, as we must, the history of Judaea and Galilee under the early empire in this category, this is a philosophical theory about the relation of the apparent to the real which hardly touches religion or conduct. If, however, we treat the contents of the Gospels in particular as mere allegory, in a sense in which we should not speak of actual historical events as mere allegory, that is a very different thing. St. John almost revels in symbolism - events for him are rich in hidden meanings - but he attaches great importance to the actual occurrence of the Incarnation. It is not difficult to see why he does so. The Incarnation teaches us that God reveals Himself most fully in the fullest and richest developments of being and actuality, in that form of life in which the processes of nature seem to culminate and converge, in the soul of the perfect man, in the soul of Christ. Moreover, the Incarnation, with the κένωσις which it involves, teaches us that Goodness does not need the accessories of Power and Omniscience in order to be divine, though the separation of Goodness from Power is only a temporary dispensation. This is the "offence of the Cross," which distinguishes Christianity from the nature-religions. And Divine Goodness, as we have said, involves Divine Self-sacrifice. "God can only make His work to be truly His own by eternally dying, sacrificing what is dearest to Him." [2] In its generalised form this high truth has been recognised even in Buddhism. "In all the world there is not one spot so large as a mustard seed, where the Buddha has not surrendered his body for the good of the creatures." [3] Here Buddha is plainly not Gautama, but the divine in man. Christians can point, with far more force, to the sacrament or symbol of this divine sacrifice in the historical Passion of the Son of God.

But the Incarnation was not terminated by the Ascension. Ritschlianism confines us to a static view of revelation, or rather compels us to see in later developments a progressive falling away from the primitive purity of the revelation. Christ Himself understood His task differently. He knew well the insuperable difficulties of imparting His whole message to such childish minds as those of His disciples. How much He held back as manifestly beyond their comprehension, we shall never know. How much was uttered only to be forgotten or misunderstood, we cannot tell. "Again and again we find a sigh of weariness, a groaning in spirit over the incurable carnality of man's thought: 'Oh fools, and slow of heart to believe,' or, 'Are ye yet without understanding?' or, 'So long have I been with you, and yet thou sayest, Show us the Father,' or the quiet despair of 'It is enough,' when they offer Him the two swords, as though explanation was hopeless with such childish listeners." [4] No wonder that He steadily looked forward to the dispensation of the Spirit, which "was not yet," [5] to carry on and complete his revelation. He had still many things to say to the human race, but they could not bear them then.

It is not, then, in the Gospels only that we are to look for the record of the Incarnation and for its fruits. The Church was meant to be the depositary of the divine indwelling; and though the public policy of the Church may seem to display few signs of divine guidance, the lives of the saints do not disappoint us. The Christ whom the Church has worshipped is a fuller and richer revelation of the Son of God than the Jesus whom the Evangelists have depicted. There is no necessity for drawing contrasts between the Christ of history and the Christ of faith, as if faith and fact could possibly be independent of each other. We are not driven to acknowledging *comme deux Christs* with Loisy. The Christ of the Church is the same Christ as Jesus of Nazareth; but the Church understands who and what He is more fully than those could do who walked with Him on the shores of Gennesaret. It was expedient for us that He should go away.

The revelation is even yet incomplete. The Church is not, as a popular hymn asserts, "far down the ages now, her journey well-nigh done." In all probability, her journey is only just begun. Two thousand years is as nothing to the period which probably remains for the human race. We should look forward more than we do. The early Church always looked forward, not back. St. Paul has described for us his own attitude, "forgetting those things which are behind, and reaching forward to those things which are before," and it is plain from all his Epistles that this was indeed his consistent habit, even to the extent of cherishing illusions about the approaching return of Christ to earth. All through the first century, it was the Parousia, rather than the Galilean ministry, that filled men's thoughts. When this hope faded, or rather when it was obliged to make for itself other forms, dreams of the *Civitas Dei,* hopes and fears of the last judgment, took its place. Those who say the Lord's Prayer "with the understanding" every day, can hardly help looking ever forward for the coming of the kingdom and the perfect fulfilment of the will of God.

I have ventured to say that the twentieth century should know more of Christ than the first. In looking back at the history of Christian thought, how strange have been the garments in which that sacred figure has successively been draped! Every age, every nation has shown a pathetic eagerness to trace in Him the lineaments of its own ideal. Have we not seen Him depicted as an ascetic, as a warrior, as a high-priest, and more recently as *le bon sans-culotte,* as a socialist? Is it disrespectful to say that the Christ of Renan is a Frenchman, the Christ of Seeley's *Ecce Homo* an Englishman, the Christ of some recent German biographies a German of the new type? There is a true instinct behind these naive distortions of a historical figure. Christ is the universal man, the ideal of humanity; and it is right that He should be "crowned with many crowns," as each nation and each century invests Him with its own ideal attributes.

But it is not enough to reverence Christ as the ideal man. That is not the Christianity which converted Europe. The orthodox Greek fathers were not afraid to say, "Christ was made man that we might become God." The author of the Epistle to Diognetus (one of the first to use such language) says that "Christ is ever begotten anew in the hearts of the saints." St. Augustine says, "Let us rejoice and return thanks that we have been made not only Christians, but Christ. Wonder and rejoice! We have been made Christ." I do not advocate such language as this. I am very glad that modern theology has abandoned the language of deification, which is not scriptural, and which always indicates, I think, either too low an idea of God, or too high an idea of man. The former was the error of the Greek fathers, for whom (as I have shown in an appendix to my Bampton lectures) θεός was a very fluid concept. The latter was the error of the medieval mystics who used similar language. But union with the glorified Christ is the essence of Christianity. The belief that the Word of God becomes incarnate in the hearts of the faithful is the very centre of Christian philosophy. It has been well expressed by the late Professor Wallace, of Oxford, who approaches the religious problems of Christianity from the side of metaphysics. "The great deed that seems to emerge as the life of Christ is the bringing into one of God and man: the discovery that the supernatural is in the natural, the spiritual in the physical: the eternal life as the truth and basis of this: God manifest in the flesh: removal of the partition wall between God and man; the immanence of the divine, not as a new and imported element in human life, but as the truth and life in life. And the practical corollary is twofold first, it is absolute peace in believing. The veil is rent away which in days of ignorance hid God and made Him an unknown God; clad Him in thick darkness and terrors of the mount, saw Him invisible in excess of light, heard Him whispering indistinctly in the separate events of history a factor incalculable, mysterious, awful. But there is another side. The absolute freedom of the Christian man is absolute allegiance to God. His freedom is from the tyranny of partial claims, individual desires and objects; and it is won by identification with the universal. It is here that *humility* comes in. Humility is the sense of solidarity and community; the controlling and regulating power of the consciousness that we are not our own, but God's and our neighbour's. Finally, the most practical corollary is love. There are two great commandments on which hinge all the law and the prophets. The first bids love God; the second, love the neighbour as self. These are not separate, and cannot be balanced one against the other. God, self, and neighbour, form an indissoluble Trinity." [6]

[1] H. More, *Mastix his Letter to a Friend,* p. 306.
[2] R. L. Nettleship.
[3] L. Hearn, *Kokoro,* p. 219.
[4] Petre, *The Soul's Orbit,* p. 70.
[5] John vii. 39.
[6] W. Wallace, *Lectures and Essays,* p. 49-51 (abridged).

Four - The Problem of Personality

I have reminded you that neither our Lord Himself, nor the Christians of the Apostolic age, nor the Greek and Roman fathers and bishops who drew up the Creeds, had any word for personality, or felt the want of any word. I have shown what confusion was introduced into Christian theology by the fact that ὑπόστασις and persona by no means corresponded in meaning; and I have also shown that when these words were used of the "Persons" of the Trinity, neither of them meant anything like what we mean by "Personality." This much is, I suppose, generally admitted; but the consequences of the admission as regards human personality are not sufficiently recognised. When Christian philosophy in our time makes the conception of *personality* the foundation of its whole metaphysical and ethical structure, when Christian writers call themselves "personal idealists" and the like, we must remind them that they are at best translating Christian theology into an alien dialect. And if our object is to understand the faith once delivered to the saints, and not to reconstruct it, it is a serious matter to introduce a word of such importance - almost a new category - which was neither used nor consciously missed by ancient thought.

When we read the utterances on personality of so representative a modern philosopher as Professor Seth (Pringle Pattison), we cannot fail to see what an entirely different world we are in from that of early Christian theology. "Each self," says the Scottish philosopher, "is a unique existence, which is perfectly impervious to other selves - impervious in a fashion of which the impenetrability of matter is a faint analogue." I do not quite know what "the impenetrability of matter" means; but let us just compare this doctrine of impervious selves, *solida pollentia simplicitate*, with the absolutely fluid conception of personality which we find in the New Testament. Jesus Christ was seriously suspected of being Elijah or Jeremiah, or even John Baptist, who had just been beheaded. And unless we are willing to sacrifice the whole of the deepest and most spiritual teaching of St. Paul and St. John, unless we are prepared to treat all the solemn language of the New Testament about the solidarity of the body and its members, the vine and its branches, as fantastic and misleading metaphor, we must assert roundly that this notion of "impervious" spiritual atoms is flatly contrary to Christianity. The result of holding such a view is the mutilation and distortion of the whole body of Christian theology. It involves the strangest and most unethical theories about the Atonement. Doctrines of forensic transactions between the Persons of the Trinity, of vicarious punishments inflicted or accepted by God, of fictitious imputation of merit, all come from attempting to reconcile the theory of impervious atoms with a tradition which knows nothing of them. As for the sacramental doctrine of the Catholic Church, it is not held by the majority of those who belong to the school of "personal idealism," and to me at least it seems wholly incompatible with it. If "eating the flesh of Christ and drinking His blood" has any meaning at all, it symbolises something much closer than an ethical harmony of wills between ourselves and God. It means nothing less than what our Prayer-book says that it means - that "we are one with Christ and Christ with us." This conception presented no difficulties in the ancient Church, because the doctrine of impervious personalities had not then been thought of. To those who hold this doctrine, nothing seems to be left of the Eucharist except a solemn commemoration of Christ's death, and a common meal as a pledge of brotherly love. The Eucharist, in fact, ceases to be a "sacrament" in the accepted sense of the word. For the mystical union of which it is the sacrament is, according to this philosophy, an impossibility and an absurdity. The Church, however, established and maintained the Eucharist as the outward form of a truth which has never, I think, been better stated than by Bishop Westcott, in his Commentary on St. John (xvii. 21). "The true unity of believers, like the unity of Persons in the blessed Trinity, is offered as something far more than a mere moral unity of purpose, feeling, affection; it is, in some mysterious mode which we cannot apprehend, a vital unity. In this sense it is the symbol of a higher type of life, in which each constituent being is a conscious element in the being of a vast whole. In 'the life,' and in 'the life' only, each individual life is able to attain perfection." Mr. R. L. Nettleship, trying to picture to himself what the world would be like if this kinship of human souls in Christ were universally recognised and acted upon, says: "Suppose that all human beings felt habitually to each other as they now do occasionally to those they love best. All the pain of the world would be swallowed up in doing good. So far as we can conceive of such a state, it would be one in which there would be no 'individuals' at all, but an universal being in and for another; where being took the form of consciousness, it would be the consciousness of another which was also oneself - a *common* consciousness. Such would be the *atonement* of the world."

The modern conception of rigid impenetrable personality seems to have its historical beginning with Kant. At any rate, the idea of a person as a self-conscious and self-determining individual, and as such an end to himself, had never been so much emphasised before. From that time the supreme importance attached to the subject-object relation has profoundly affected all philosophical thinking, and often, as I venture to think, in an unfortunate manner. The distinction between subject and object cannot be absolute; otherwise our very theory of knowledge makes knowledge impossible. And yet it is just its pretensions to be absolute for which most people value it. Nine people out of ten, when they speak about subject and object, mean by subject the supposed individual soul, and by object the supposed real world perceived by the senses. They then think that they have a respectable philosophical basis for the crude antithesis between "self" and "not self," which it should be the common task of philosophy and religion to reduce to its proper insignificance.

For what is the evidence for the unity of self-consciousness, so often treated as axiomatic? "The identity of the subject of inward experience," says Lotze, "is all that we require." But can we claim that we do so know ourselves as identical? We have no direct knowledge of the permanent Ego as object. The self that we partially know is a series of feelings, and acts of will, and thoughts. The unity which we assume to underlie and connect these states is certainly not given; it is even known to us not to be a fact, but an ideal. Most assuredly the antithesis between the one and the many is not the same as that between subject and object. Our mental states give us the whole gamut from the one to the many; and so does the external world. In fact no personal experience can claim to be more direct and intimate than that of an inner division of the personality - that experience, sometimes painful, sometimes blissful, which leads St. Paul to cry, at one time, "wretched man that I am!" and at another, "I live, yet not I, but Christ liveth in me."

When the Neoplatonists lay down the rule ἕνα γενέσθαι ἄνθρωπον δεῖ - "a man ought to be one" they are setting up an ideal which is not, and never will be completely, a matter of experience. In their system and those of their Christian disciples, unification of the personality is a gradual process, coincident with our growth in grace. The obstacle to its achievement is the clinging taint of selfishness and self-consciousness. In some lives this obstacle appears mainly as an impediment; in others the collision assumes the more tragic form of a struggle between the forces of good and evil for the possession of a man's soul. There have been men brilliantly endowed by nature who have carried with them from the cradle to the grave the almost intolerable burden of a divided personality. The miserable lives of Swift, Rousseau, and Schopenhauer appall us by the juxtaposition of splendid intellectual virtues with moral weakness and even turpitude which they present. The life of Samuel Taylor Coleridge is a melancholy but less repulsive example, exhibiting the same combination of intellectual strength and moral debility. It is not for us to determine which was the true man, in these cases or in such inconsistent lives as that of Seneca, or Petrarch, whose *De Contemptu Mundi* is in flagrant contradiction with what we know of his life. But the majority of good Christians harmonise the discordant strings in their souls without such terrible inward struggles. With them, the unification of personality is gradually effected by quieter methods. I have argued elsewhere [1] that sudden conversion, though a fairly common phenomenon even when no suggestion has been applied from outside, and the rule rather than the exception when this kind of stimulus has been applied, is not the commonest or most regular method of spiritual growth. I know that the valuable researches of Starbuck and others in this country point to a different conclusion; but unless the typical mental and spiritual development in adolescence differs widely on the two sides of the Atlantic, I feel sure that Starbuck's statistics are misleading, being drawn too much from sects which teach sudden conversion, and lead boys and girls to expect it. In my own experience, I have never come across a case of sudden conversion at all resembling the crisis which the Methodists consider normal. And even where it occurs, it by no means follows that the change is as sudden as the consciousness of it. The transformation of our personality, whereby Christ becomes the form of our life, must surely always be a gradual process. At a certain stage it may present itself to our consciousness as a sudden upheaval. But this period of storm and stress, if it comes upon us at all, generally gives way to a more peaceful state, in which we are able to co-operate willingly in God's purposes in and for us, and to overcome some of the contradictions which formerly distressed us.

Now will any one venture to say that this spiritual progress consists in an increasing consciousness of the barrier which separates the thinking subject from all other subjects? Let us consider how the matter stands. The Christian revelation, it will be generally admitted, was the beginning of a new era in man's knowledge of himself and of God. It is often maintained or assumed that this deepening of thought, with the new delicacy of self-knowledge with which it was connected, resulted in the abandonment of vague pantheistic notions about impersonal Mind and Soul, and in the growing conviction that souls are impenetrable, self-existing, spiritual atoms, as they appear in the philosophy of Lotze and his disciples. But this is at best only half the truth. From the very first, our Lord pointed out the path which Christian psychology must follow. It involved the acceptance of a paradox, of an apparent contradiction. Man has a ψυχή, a soul, a personality, and yet it is not his indefectibly - it may be lost; nay, in a sense it is not his yet at all, but has to be "acquired in patience" (Luke xxi. 19). In other words, personality is, as I have said, an ideal; not a given fact. We are to gain, acquire our personality in patience. And the paradox lies in this, that the way to gain it is to lose it. This maxim has been rightly emphasised by many writers as the very kernel of the Christian revelation. And how does a man "lose his soul" so as to gain it? By submitting to be put to death as a martyr? By "losing his life," as the Authorised Version translates it? Certainly not; the corresponding clause, "he that wishes to save his ψυχή shall lose it," precludes this interpretation. Does it refer to eternal life? How then could it be said that the Christian is willing to lose his ψυχή. No; to be willing to lose our ψυχή must mean to forget ourselves entirely, to cease to revolve round our own selfish interests, to pass out freely into the great life of the world, constructing our universe on a Christocentric or cosmocentric basis, not a self-centred one. To do this is to lose and then find ourselves. "The way to get to God is to let oneself go as much as possible into the unity which one potentially is, while all evil and failure is a form of self-assertion." [2] "Know thyself" is a great maxim, but he who would know himself must know himself in God. To attempt to find self (the individual) without God (the universal), says Professor Ritchie, is to find - the devil. The individual assumed by the psychologist, and by the common political and ethical theories, is a half-way abstraction of the ordinary understanding, a bastard product of bad metaphysics and bad science. Christianity, as we have seen, from the very first rejected it.

This paradox of the spiritual life implies that the universal and individual are abstractions, each of which would collapse without the other. Indeed, the union of individuality and universality in a single manifestation forms the cardinal point in personality. The spiritual life consists in a double movement - of expansion and intension. But the intensification of life - the acquisition of a deeper and stronger individuality - is not to be the immediate aim of our conscious efforts. These are to spread outward and upward. We are to throw ourselves heartily into great and worthy interests, to forget ourselves and lose ourselves in them (the popular phraseology is valuable as indicating what we seem to ourselves to be doing), to *become* what we are interested in. As Goethe says:-

"Nur wo du bist, sei alles, immer kindlich;
So bist du allea, bist unüberwindlich."

The transfigured self that we acquire by thus living a larger, impersonal life, is so different from the original self with which we began our upward course, that St. Paul, thinking of his own experiences, cannot regard them as the same. "Of such an one will I glory," he says, referring to his "visions and revelations," "but of myself I will not" (ὑπὲρ δὲ ἐμαυτοῦ οὔ). [3] Thus Christianity accepts the Platonic distinction between the higher and the lower self, and agrees with Plato that the higher self is born of influences which belong to the eternal world, the supernatural source of truth and goodness. [4]

This law of growth through the clash and union of opposites runs all through the Christian experience. There is no self-expenditure without self-enrichment, no self-enrichment without self-expenditure. The ideals of self-culture and of self-sacrifice, so far from being hopelessly contra-dictory, as even such acute thinkers as Bradley and A. E. Taylor have sup-posed, are inseparable, and unrealisable except as two aspects of the same process. Any one who tries to attain complete self-expression - to build his pyramid of existence, as Goethe put it, as an isolated individual, is certain to fail ignominiously. The self that he is trying to bring to per-fection is a mere abstraction, a figment of his imagination. And, converse-ly, any one who lived a purely external life, with no inner soul-centre to which all experiences must be related, would be nothing either. Our uni-fying consciousness is the type and the copy of the all-unifying con-sciousness of God. Our individuality is a shadow of His.

Those who are afraid of a philosophy which seems at first sight to de-personalise man should reflect that this is the philosophy which attaches the greatest importance to unity as a supreme attribute of God, and sets out the attainment of unity or personality by ourselves as the goal of all our striving. Not that our aim is to attain an individuality separate from or independent of the life of God. Such an aspiration would be philosoph-ically absurd and religiously impious. In most relations of life there are few better moral maxims than this of Fichte: "There is but one virtue, to forget oneself as a person; one vice, to remember oneself." The *Theologia Germanica* has rightly apprehended the meaning of our Lord's frequent protestations that He was merely sent by the Father, and neither did nor said anything of Himself. "Christ's human nature was so utterly bereft of self, as no man's ever was, and was nothing else but a house and habitation of God. Neither of that in Him which belonged to God, nor of that which was a living human creature and habitation of God, did He, as man, claim anything for His own. His human nature did not even take unto itself the Godhead, whose dwelling it was; there was no claiming of anything, no seeking nor desire, saving that what was due might be rendered to the Godhead; and He did not call this very desire His own." "The self, the I, the Me, and the like, all belong to the evil spirit, and therefore it is that he is an evil spirit. Behold, one or two words can utter all that has been said in many words: Be simply and wholly bereft of self." "In true light and true love there neither is nor can remain any I, Me, Mine, Thou, Thine, and the like, but that light perceiveth and knoweth that there is a good which is above all good, and that all good things are of one substance in the one good, and that without that one there is no good thing. And therefore where this light is, the man's end and aim is not this or that, Me or Thee, or the like, but only the One, who is neither I nor Thou, this nor that, but is above all I and Thou, this and that, and in Him all goodness is loved as one good, according to that saying, All in One as One, and One in All as All, and one and all good is loved through the One in One, and for the sake of the One, for the love that man hath to the One." This treatise makes short work of the "will-worship" which is now treated with so much respect by philosophers. "Be assured, he that helpeth a man to his own will, helpeth him to the worst that he can. Nothing burneth in hell but self-will. Therefore it hath been said, Put off thine own will, and there will be no more hell. As long as a man is seeking his own good, he doth not yet seek what is best for him, and he will never find it. For a man's highest good would be and is truly this, that he should not seek himself and his own things, *nor be his own end in any respect, either in things spiritual or in things natural,* but should seek only the praise and glory of God, and His holy will." "He that hateth his soul for my sake shall keep it unto life eternal." The words of our Lord are quite as strong, even stronger, than those of this mediaeval mystic. I fear we have most of us travelled a long way from them, both in our habits of thought and in our lives.

I should not have drawn attention so strongly to the growing tendency in modern thought towards individualism and subjectivism if the matter were only one of speculative or academic interest. But it has a direct bearing on religious belief and even on conduct. Lotze, the protagonist of personal idealism, in this as in other ways seems to have devoted his brilliant abilities to justifying the naive philosophy of the man in the street. The popularity of such views in the English-speaking countries is not surprising. The Anglo-Saxon is by temperament and training an individualist. He has been brought up to think that his main business is to assert himself, to make his fortune in this world or the next, or in both. He likes to believe in a God who is an individual like himself, and who, like himself, can be a partner in a transaction. Justice, for him, means equitable and kindly treatment of individuals, and can have no other meaning. The constitution of the world is the product of acts of will, not a system of laws to be discovered and obeyed. In my next lecture I shall discuss the question whether this sort of Personal Idealism is in accordance with what we know about the world in which we live. It is, in any case, very near what most people would like to be true. It is the kind of world which "the will to believe," if it were entrusted with the task of world-construction, might be expected to produce. The difficulties which it introduces into the region of Christian faith are enormous. For instance, the doctrine of the Trinity becomes an incomprehensible and manifestly self-contradictory piece of word-jugglery, because a Person is by definition one who cannot share his being with another.

When our Lord said, "Believe Me that I am in My Father, and ye in Me," He was, on this theory, either using an extravagant oriental metaphor, or saying nothing. Our theory of God, if we follow these guides, must be either an abstract monotheism or polytheism. The latter theory has not yet been openly advocated by the school which we are criticising, but it is plainly more in harmony with their views about the independent plurality of human spirits than any form of monotheism. The relations between God and man must be conceived of in a widely different manner from that of the New Testament (for we need not separate the theology of St. Paul and St. John from that of the other books). God must be a Spirit among other spirits, not the deepest life and final home of all spirits. Such a conception of the Deity, if counterbalanced, as it should be, by that of a personal devil, is a useful piece of symbolism for the conscience in its struggle with sin; but if it is offered us as a metaphysical truth, we can only say that such a God would not be God at all. And as regards the relation of human beings to each other, this theory of impervious personal identity destroys the basis on which Christian love is supported. We are bidden to love our neighbours as ourselves, because we are all one in Christ Jesus. Is this also a mere metaphor, an example of oriental hyperbole? It was not intended to be so taken. It was the good news of the Gospel that those barriers, which are now solemnly declared to be for ever unsurmountable, are non-existent. Christian love is not sentimental philanthropy; it is the practical recognition of a natural and positive fact - namely, that we are all so bound up together, as sharers in the same life and members of the same body, that selfishness is a disease and a blunder which can only result in mortal injury both to the offending limb and to the whole body.

The Stoics used to say that the selfish man is a cancer in the universe. A cancer is caused by unchecked proliferation of cellular tissue by one organ independently of the rest of the body. The parallel is therefore scientifically exact. The revelation that "God is love" means that love has its origin in the eternal and universal side of our nature. It is the glad recognition of a deeper unity, beneath our superficial isolation. Of all human experiences, it is the one which most uplifts us and brings us closest to God, just because it rends from top to bottom the veil of separation between human beings: it opens a wide breach in the middle wall of partition which keeps us apart from each other, and therefore also apart from God. And, on the contrary, selfishness and self-consciousness, which in the Gospels is hardly less severely dealt with than selfishness, are at every stage "that which letteth, and which will let, till it be taken out of the way." It is in the nature of things that we can do no injury, dictated by selfishness, without suffering a corresponding loss. "The soul which falls short of the law of universal respect, and treats one of the least of things as if it too were not God's creature, is struck with a withering of which the natural issue is death." [5] I need not remind you how dear this doctrine was to Emerson. "The thief steals from himself; the swindler swindles himself. You can do no wrong without suffering wrong. No man ever had a point of pride that was not injurious to him."

One very great gain which would result from this way of looking at things would be the silencing of importunate doubts about theodicy. It is, or should be plain that we can prefer no claim to personal justice, compensation, or reward, either in this life or the next, without *ipso facto* putting ourselves out of relation with the God of love revealed by Christ, and taking as our guide what the *Theologia Germanica* calls "the false light," that will-of-the-wisp which draws us astray with its perpetual "I and Thou," "Mine and Thine." That justice will be done we may be absolutely sure. We are more sure that God is just than of anything else in the world. But the moment we begin to weigh the claims of A and B, especially if we ourselves are A, we enter a region in which the divine justice can have nothing to say to us except, "What hast thou that thou didst not receive?" If we would not be judged, we must not appear as litigants before the Almighty.

The hypothesis of a racial self, with a higher degree of personal life than that of individual men and women, is an attractive one, and one which might easily be brought into connection with the Logos-theology. Something like it is familiar to all students of Emerson, under the name of the Over-soul. The Over-soul is his name for the unity within which every man's particular being is contained and made one with all others, "the common heart of which all sincere conversation is the worship, to which all right action is submission. All goes to show that the soul in man is not the intellect, nor the will, but the master of the intellect and the will, is the background of our being, in which they lie. When the soul, whose organ he is, breathes through his intellect, it is genius; when it breathes through his will, it is virtue; when it flows through his affection, it is love. The blindness of the intellect begins, when it would be something of itself. The weakness of the will begins when the individual would be something of himself." The Over-soul is the perceiver and revealer of truth, and its manifestations of its own nature we call revelation. This is the regular mystical psychology, but Plotinus, as we have seen, ranked νοῦς above ψυχή, and might have preferred the former name for the Oversoul, as having more dignity. Christians have generally preferred the word "Spirit," which indeed seems by far the best. The Spirit is the higher life of humanity, which keeps alive the results of its experience, its hardly won wisdom, its knowledge of good and evil, its faith, its hope, and its love. It holds steadily before it the ideal which the human race was meant to realise, the Kingdom of God which it is to set up upon earth. The old theology was not afraid to identify the Spirit, in its activities, with the *Church.*

We need not reject this identification, for the spiritual life is most fully realised in the life of the community. But perhaps we shall extend the frontiers of "the Church" rather further than those who first claimed it as the mouthpiece of the Holy Ghost.

The doctrine of the Over-soul, like the older doctrine of the Logos, obliges us to take our choice between monism and pluralism. "We must either reject the very idea of the Absolute with the Pragmatists, and be content with an experience that is not a unity, a world that is not a cosmos, a moral law whose authority is relative, and a God who is finite, or else we must be prepared to assert the presence of the Absolute in all experience, as the truth which knowledge is progressively attaining, as the good which is being realised in morality, as the reality in which the religious consciousness finds its fulfilment and satisfaction." [6] The choice lies between a radical empiricism and a thorough-going monism, as Professor W. James says. We must choose between the anthropocentric and the cosmocentric points of view.

Such a monad ism as that of Leibnitz is no improvement on frank pluralism, though it professes to be a compromise between pluralism and monism. The spiritual atoms of which his world are composed are said to form a system "ideally," *i.e.* for the mind of an all-wise spectator. There is no reciprocal action between the monads, but a pre-established harmony which is due to the will of God, who, as in most philosophical systems of this type, is not really God, but a finite spirit. Leibnitz seems to have *started* with the assumption that human souls are impenetrable, indiscerptible atoms, and then to have built up his theory of monads to account for it. And when we turn from him to Lotze, it is difficult to see how his monistic conclusion, edifying as it no doubt is, in any way follows from the rest of his philosophy, which leaves us with a world of spirits entirely separate from each other. "What pluralism does, consciously or unconsciously, is to separate the unity of the world from its multiplicity. The multiplicity is supposed to be grounded in the ultimate nature of the real things themselves, their unity as a system, if they really are a system, to be imposed upon them from without. We cannot rest finally content with a statement of this kind, which leaves the plurality and the systematic unity of the real world side by side as independent unconnected facts." [7] If we say that the world consists of a number of independent "spirits," who constitute a moral kingdom in virtue of their common relation to

God, this relation is a fact as much as their separateness, and a fact fatal to pluralism. Their union is not an external relation, but the deepest truth about them. We are then left with an irreducible contradiction. From a pluralistic hypothesis to a monistic conclusion there is no road.

I do not wish to deny that there is an element of truth in this jealous adherence to the doctrine of impervious spiritual atoms. In our struggles with temptation, it is important to keep in the foreground the doctrine of personal responsibility. I have no doubt that the popularity of pluralism is due to the fact that it is believed to safeguard certain moral and religious interests. It has been urged that it alone gives us "a real God" and "real moral freedom." Now "a real God" is just what this theory does not give us, but only a limited struggling spirit - a "magnified and non-natural" conscience. That the battle with evil is a real one, and that God is on the side of good, are truths for the moral consciousness; but to make this faculty and its cravings, with their specific determinations, the sole constitutive principle of reality, is to mutilate experience. I have already shown, I think, that the deepest and most characteristic doctrines of Christianity are unintelligible and incredible on a pluralistic hypothesis, while the whole of mysticism, which has always supplied the life-blood of religion, is dried up by it at the source. If pragmatical considerations are to be admitted at all in dealing with metaphysical problems, it would be easy to show that they by no means tell only on the side of pluralism or "personal idealism."

The unity which we assert, whether of the human spirit or of the real world, is not a mere numerical expression. It is not the kind of unity which many of the mystics have sought to reach by the method of negation - stripping their souls bare in their search for the infinite, and finding at last not infinity but zero. It is not the unity which consists in the mere aggregate of parts. In a mere aggregate there is no principle of unity inherent in the parts. We choose to collect the pieces, and think of them together. But this is no real unity. Nor can we rightly think of the human soul, in Stoical fashion, as *divinae particula aurae*. This is nearer the truth than the hypothesis of mere aggregation, but it is not the Christian view of our relation to God, and it is philosophically unsatisfactory. For in a composition of this kind, the whole cannot exist without the parts, whereas the parts might continue to exist, though not as parts, without the whole. God, on the other hand, does not depend on His creatures for His existence, but they do depend upon Him for theirs.

The figure of an organism is the truest and most instructive that we can frame, to express the relation of the Divine Logos to His creatures. It is the figure which Christ Himself chose, and which is freely used in other parts of the New Testament. Christ proclaimed Himself the true Vine (not, be it observed, the root or stem of the tree, but the Vine itself), of which we are the branches. The whole is not the resultant of the parts, but their living unity. The members depend for their existence on the life of the whole. If it dies, they die; if they are severed, they die and are no more; for, as Aristotle says, a severed hand is no longer a hand, except "equivocally." Nevertheless, it is well for us to remember that the metaphor of an organism, valuable as it is, is only a metaphor, and an inadequate one, as all metaphors must be which seek to express spiritual truths. It is inadequate, because it does something less than justice to the claims of human personality. A "member" can hardly be said to exist in any degree for itself, and still less can the whole be said to exist for the sake of the members. But the human soul has an independent value, though not an independent existence. We may say, if we will, that the unity which binds us to the Logos is that of a *system,* in which parts and whole are equally real; or we may remember and utilise the sentence already quoted from Proclus, that the highest kind of whole is that in which the whole and its parts are "woven together." The psychological basis of our doctrine is that in our nature we have correspondences with every grade of reality, from the lowest to the highest. There is therefore a uniqueness, a singleness, in our nature, an image of the uniqueness and singleness of God. At this apex of our being we have an inkling of a fully personal life, which we may claim in virtue of the very severity of our monism. We believe in God, not in a God, and "there is none beside Him"; but we could not have this belief about Him if there were not the germs of a fully personal nature in ourselves.

This conception of a soul-centre, through which we are in contact with God Himself, though in an unspeakably dim, remote, and faint degree, seems to me a valuable one, because it safeguards what is true in our aspirations after separate individuality, and asserts the fundamentally teleological character of these aspirations. The practical difficulty in grasping the conception is due to the fact that spiritual things are not outside or inside each other. The inevitable spatial symbols are very troublesome. But we should try to make it our own, for it is the true philosophy of the Christian religion. "Christus in omnibus *totus*" supplies the necessary corrective of the "whole and part" metaphor, and also of the "organic" metaphor. The gifts of the Spirit are divided: "Non omnia possumus omnes" - but Christ is not divided.

[1] *Truth and Falsehood in Religion,* Lecture III.
[2] R. L. Nettleship.
[3] 2 Cor. xii. 5.
[4] See Royce, *The World and the Individual,* vol. ii. 250, who well shows the psychological basis of the "two selves."
[5] Wallace, *Lectures and Essays,* p. 175.
[6] Professor Henry Jones, in *Hibbert Journal,* October, 1903.
[7] Taylor, *Elements of Metaphysics,* p. 89.

Five - Thought and Will

One of the strangest phenomena of our time is the strong current of anti-intellectualism in philosophy and theology, contrasted with the unbroken confidence in purely intellectual methods which is apparent in all other branches of human thought. This is not really a sceptical age. It has staked its all on the unity and continuity of nature, and the possibility of a coherent knowledge of nature as a system. It has based its labours on this assumption, and has reaped a rich harvest by doing so. In all the natural sciences great and unmistakable progress has been made; and each new discovery has added fresh justification for the trust in nature and the trust in reason, on which the researches which led to it were founded. This is not an age in which mankind will renounce either the right or the duty to search for the truth; it is not an age in which suggestions that the truth is unimportant, or unknowable, or subject to revision by "authority" (whatever that means) are likely to be regarded favourably. If we take up any scientific work, even of a controversial character, we are at once struck by the wholehearted desire to form a judgment strictly on the evidence, by the absence of rhetoric and special pleading, and the confident assumption that it must be good for us to know the facts as they are, whether they square with our preconceived notions of the fitness of things or not.

And yet when we turn to the most important subject of all - whether we call it the knowledge of ultimate truth, or the knowledge of God we find that with many writers no effort is spared to pour contempt on the methods which in every other field are held in honour. Never, perhaps, in the whole history of philosophy has there been so much open profession of what Plato calls μισολογία, hatred of reason, as we find in what is now the most self-confident and aggressive school of philosophy. In other times there have been fiery ascetics and devout recluses who have scorned the pride of intellect and dwelt much upon the theme that God has chosen the weak things of the world to confound the wise; but never before have acute thinkers so rejoiced to trample on the pretensions of the intellect, and to lend the weight of their authority to the rehabilitation of mere prejudices. How widespread and influential this anti-intellectualist movement is may be gathered by enumerating a few names of those who have joined it. In philosophy, not to mention the will-philosophy of the pessimists Schopenhauer and Von Hartmann, the tendency of whose writings is, on the whole, not anti-intellectualist, we have Lotze, who positively parades his misology, stigmatising thought as "a tool," "a means," the products of which "have no real significance." Lotze carries his anti-intellectualism much further than Kant. The latter, as is well known, examined the pretensions of the speculative reason, and concluded that they must be abated. He even says, "I must abolish knowledge to make room for belief." But in his philosophy the cleft is still a rift *within* the intelligence. The dualism thus set up would be eliminated if the reason, the highest of the intellectual powers, could be made consistent with itself. The successors of Kant, notably Hegel, strove to overcome this inner discord. But in the philosophy of Lotze, the cleft is not within the intelligence, but between the intellectual and emotional faculties. The dualism with which he leaves us is thus of a far more intractable kind, and can be only terminated by the complete subjugation of thought to will and feeling. In this country, as you know, there are many distinguished advocates of pluralism and pragmatism, such as Professor Howison of California, and Professor William James, who seems willing to accept even the most extreme and startling consequences of his theory - the rehabilitation of pure chance, and an apotheosis of the irrational. Even Professor Royce, in spite of his half sympathy with absolutism, and his desire to deal fairly and appreciatively with mysticism and allied forms of thought, deliberately subordinates thought to will.

In England, Professor Ward, of Cambridge, has drawn the sword against naturalism as well as agnosticism; and Oxford has produced a band of "Personal Idealists," some of whom proclaim the virtues of pragmatism and subjectivism with an almost blatant persistency and assurance.

Distinguished amateurs in philosophy, like Mr. A. J. Balfour, have joined in the fray, exalting "authority" above "reason," and attempting once more, like Pascal and Mansel, to base religious belief on the extreme of scepticism. Mr. Benjamin Kidd achieved a considerable though brief notoriety by turning Buckle's fundamental theory of human progress clean upside down, and arguing that intellectual superiority has no survival value. In poetry we have Robert Browning, the robustest intellect among the poets of his generation, who, in the latter part of his life especially, gave way to a strange μισολογία. in matters of faith, of which the strongest example may be found in *La Saisiaz*. In theology the reaction against intellectualism has affected apologetics both among Catholics and Protestants. Liberal Catholicism is decidedly pragmatist in type, as indeed was Newman's theology on one side. Loisy and Tyrrell are willing to allow criticism a free hand in the investigation of Christian origins and biblical problems, just because all the verdicts of science are discredited in advance, as based upon mere facts, and therefore irrelevant in matters of faith. For Tyrrell, the spirit-world is the will-world: the words are used by him interchangeably. For Loisy, no conclusions as to facts can affect the truth of a single dogma, precisely because facts are facts, while dogmas are representative ideas of faith. If facts are so unimportant as this, it would seem to be hardly worthwhile for any one to give his life to the investigation of them. Protestant theology has long been deeply affected by the same tendencies. Ritschl separates faith and belief as carefully as Loisy separates faith and fact: and the result seems to be much the same. The subjective impression of Christ made upon us by the Gospel narrative is the important thing.; Metaphysical problems are set aside as irrelevant and useless. Among Ritschl's followers, none exhibits this side of his theology in a more glaring light than Herrmann, the author of the *Communion of the Christian with God,* which has been translated into English. In this strange book we find in an exaggerated form the hostility to mysticism which is also apparent in Harnack and other Protestant theologians in Germany. Harnack thinks that any mystic who does not become a Romanist is a dilettante, and Herrmann argues with vehemence that "mysticism is [Roman] Catholic piety." If it were not manifestly absurd to confine mysticism to any one section of the Christian world, it would be a somewhat less perverse misstatement to say that mysticism is Protestant piety. For the essence of Protestantism is, I suppose, the right and duty of private judgment, the belief in individual inspiration.

Protestantism, in fact, is the democracy of religion, the claim of every one to live by the light that God has given him. And the mystics, as Professor Royce has well said, are the only thorough-going empiricists. Catholicism has tolerated and used mysticism, but has never viewed it without suspicion, and has often persecuted it. It is not to be expected that the inheritor of the traditions of the Roman Empire should view with favour a type of religion which puts the inner light above human authority, and finds its sacraments everywhere. To say, then, that "mysticism is Catholic piety," is to show that the speaker entirely fails to understand both mysticism and Catholicism. So fundamental a misunderstanding prepares us for strange views about the relations of faith and knowledge. It appears, however, that according to some of this school, the two have no relations. The intellect takes cognisance of facts, religion has to do only with the moral ideal, and these two views of the world have nothing to do with each other. "The refusal to recognise the irreducible difference that exists between the feeling of the value of goodness and the knowledge of facts may come perhaps from the relinquishment of the supramundane character of the Christian idea of God. In plain words, the Christian idea of God is lost as soon as it is not based exclusively on the moral sense of the ideal, but on a thinking contemplation of the world as well; for between the two, ideal and reality, there is an irreducible difference." "What we speak of as real in Christianity is quite different from what we speak of as real in metaphysics...To attempt to mix up the two kinds of reality is to deny that the ethical fact, in which the religious view of the world has its root, is a separate thing, not to be grasped in the general forms of being and becoming, and not within the view of metaphysics at all." [1] This astonishingly crude dualism has at least the merit of proclaiming itself to be what it is! But it is an uncomfortable symptom that Herrmann is taken seriously both in Germany and England.

In French Protestantism also a school exists, very similar to the Ritschlian, under the somewhat cumbrous name of *Symbolo-fidéisme*. Its chief founders were the late Auguste Sabatier and his friend Ménégoz. The name, which they chose as indicating the main characteristics of their position, may be expanded into two propositions. The first is that all dogmas, whether historical or theological in form, are inadequate to their object, and should not be regarded as literal statements of fact. The second is the Ritschlian formula that we are saved by our faith and not by our belief. Sabatier was a man of wide outlook, and he does not write in the service of any one theory, but he distinctly subordinates scientific and philosophical judgments to the value -judgments of religion and morality; and he worked in complete harmony with Ménégoz, who seems to be a pragmatist of an extreme type.

What are the causes of this widespread movement, which has made so many disciples in all parts of the world? We might find analogies in the history of Greek philosophy, when the great speculative systems were followed by intellectual scepticism, and increased attention to political and ethical problems. That this is a true analogy is shown by the one-sidedness of the Kantian revival. It is only the scepticism and empiricism of Kant that are admired; his rationalism has been discarded or ignored. In some ways the new school has more in common with Locke and Hume than with Kant, a resemblance which comes out strongly in the writings of Kaftan. There are many differences in these opponents of absolutism which forbid us to class them together as forming a single school of thought; but they have a bond of union in their hostility to what they call Intellectualism and in their rejection of the greater part of Hegel's contribution to philosophy. Indeed, the reaction against the so-called Panlogism of Hegel, which (it is said) leaves the *will* out of account both in God and man, was the initial motive force in the "return to Kant."

This reaction has been to a large extent fostered in the supposed interests of morality and religion. I think that, without undue optimism, we may say that there has been a growing belief in the supreme value of moral and religious truth, though at the same time some of the foundations on which it was supposed to rest have been partly shaken by the progress of knowledge. In particular, the proof from occasional Divine intervention has been discredited, while men are by no means ready to accept the naturalism which is offered them as the only alternative. From so awkward a dilemma there seems to be no escape except by abating to some extent the claims of the reason to pronounce upon the higher kinds of truth, and setting up in opposition to it some other tribunal, which shall have at least a co-ordinate authority. This tribunal can be most easily found in the moral sense or will, though it is quite possible to divest the "will to live" of any moral character in the ordinary acceptation of the .word morality, as has been done by Max Stirner and Nietzsche, or to regard it as an evil, as in the system of Schopenhauer. The religious experience has pronounced quite decisively that mere thinking does not necessarily lead to the discovery of the truth, and that our Lord's words, "If any man willeth to do His will, he shall know of the doctrine," convey a most valuable warning against the danger of relying on the speculative intellect alone to bring us to God. The proper conclusion, that religion must be loth thought out and lived out, is too often forgotten in the heat of polemics, or rejected as a compromise which strives to reconcile two incompatible ideals. In this, however, the pragmatists are false to their own principles. It is quite true that the affirmations of the practical and speculative reason, or, as the more advanced members of the school prefer to say, the judgments of fact pronounced by the reason and the judgments of value pronounced by the will, cannot be fully harmonised. But this problem is itself an intellectual one. It is an untenable position to maintain that judgments of fact and judgments of value are on such different planes that they can never come into conflict. We are continually called upon to adjust our conduct so as to satisfy both claims. So far as I can see, every judgment that we make is at once a judgment of fact and a judgment of value; we use our intellects to assign to our values their right place in the world of fact, as we use our moral sense to assign to facts their true place in the world of ethical values. Values that have no place in the world of fact are not current coin.

It is now generally recognised that religion cannot be purely rationalistic. A rationalistic faith would not be, in the higher sense, rational, because the reason, as distinct from the understanding, is bound to take account of all experience, while rationalism takes account only of logical processes. Faith may justly quarrel with reasons, though not with reason. It follows that religious doctrines claim some other kind of truth besides that which belongs to scientific laws or facts. This view of dogma was stated, too strongly, by Schopenhauer. "Everything about religion is, truly speaking, mystery. It is unjust to demand of a religion that it shall be true *sensu proprio,* and the rationalists and supernaturalists are equally absurd, both supposing that religion must be true in this sense or not at all...The rationalists are honest people but shallow heads; they have no notion of the profound meaning of the New Testament myth, and cannot get past Jewish optimism, a thing which they can understand, and which suits them. They may be compared to the Euhemerists of antiquity...Christianity is an allegory which reflects a true idea; but allegory is not itself the truth." [2]

There are many in our day who feel the half-truth of this view of dogmatic theology. They are conscious of the value of dogma, not only to the ignorant masses, for whom it is, as Schopenhauer says, an indispensable substitute for philosophy, but for themselves; and yet they cannot disguise from themselves the profound difficulty of accepting all the dogmas of their faith as literal facts in the phenomenal sphere. The answer of "neutral monism" would, I suppose, be that the value-judgments of faith and the fact-judgments of science are parallel and complementary aspects of a reality which lies behind them both. But this view makes the reconciliation a matter of bare faith, and does nothing to bring it nearer. Moreover, it gives no guidance in matters of conduct, where we wish to know whether the judgment of fact or the judgment of value is the right one for us to follow. And lastly, those who wish to conform to the teaching of the Church, and to take their part without tormenting scruples in the life and work of the Christian society, do not find the purely representative value which this theory attaches to religious symbols enough to satisfy them. And so they fly for comfort to that disparagement of the natural order and its standards of truth which is so often met with in contemporary apologetics. This new "sacrifice of the intellect" meets us, I think, in its least respectable form in Herrmann, whose peculiar apologetics we have already discussed. Since his position obviously leads to pure subjectivism, he "can make no direct answer" to the charge that religion for him is "the mere imagination of an energetic subjectivity." He bids us take confidence in the thought that "many other hearts" are also answerable for "the inexplicable audacity of faith." In fact, this German Protestant takes refuge in the *securus iudicat orbis terrarum* - of Newman his *orbis* being "many other hearts," whose votes are neither weighed nor counted. He flies to revelation, which on his principles must be of a purely external kind, since he is a declared enemy of anything like mysticism. Such a position is, as Pfleiderer says, "more prudent than reasonable," in one who rejects Catholicism. Roman Catholic apologists can urge this argument with much greater force, because for them the historic Church is the vehicle by which the Holy Ghost reveals the truth to mankind. But in this Church the mass of propositions which, purporting to be judgments of fact, are, it appears, to be understood as judgments of value or representative ideas of faith, is intolerably large. And it must be seriously questioned whether such sceptical orthodoxy can ever be the basis of a living faith, except in a few unusually constituted minds.

When the office of the reason has been reduced so far below that of the will and feelings as it is by this school, it is not surprising that people doubt whether serious thought is worth the trouble that it costs. When a man of Pascal's intellect allows himself to say: "Se moquer de philosophie, ce soit vraiment philosopher," shall not the ordinary man, conscious that, "Träumen ist leicht, und denken ist schwer," gladly excuse himself from thinking? He may make a pretence of passing his convictions through the crucible, but it is a pretence and no more. It is always tempting, when our synthetic thinking fails to keep pace with our analytic, to assume that what is denied to us as individuals must, therefore, transcend human powers altogether. How much simpler it is to "give it up," as children say, and to justify ourselves with such maxims as *Pectus facit theologum,* or "The heart has its reasons, which the intellect knows not of." The so-called conflict between the head and the heart is generally a conflict between reflective and unreflective thought, or between reason and prejudice. "The heart" is a popular judge, because it decides in favour of the defendant without hearing the prosecution.

The doctrine that "whatever helps souls is true" is a very dangerous one if taken as a practical guide. It is only the healthy appetite that relishes wholesome fare. The diseased appetite sometimes derives satisfaction from what is peculiarly injurious, but the pleasure and satisfaction which it feels are real. We need a criterion by which to test our subjective feelings of what helps us, and this criterion must be their relation to external reality. Not values simply, but the relation of values to reality, is what religion has to determine. The language of religion is the language of practical life, but its subject-matter is objective truth. And at the very heart of religion is the conviction that our reason is a reflection of the absolute

Reason, our interests identical with those of the great system of which we are a part. The rational is real, not assuredly because our thought determines reality, but because reality determines thought.

If there is any danger of this anti-intellectualism spreading beyond the sphere of philosophy and apologetics (I do not know whether there is) the result must tend towards a petrifaction of the whole body of knowledge, a state of things which history records at more periods than one. The scientific outlook upon the world is cosmocentric; that of the pragmatist is essentially anthropocentric. But the higher religion must (as even Höffding says) be grounded in "cosmical vital feeling." Otherwise, it must renounce the hope of making peace with science. Science has no quarrel with idealism; but it can make no terms with the selfish idealism - the provincialism of thought - which makes man and his interests the measure of all things. As Planck (summarised by Pfleiderer) says: "The view which apprehends all things according to their practical bearings, requires to be supplemented and corrected by the opposite, the purely scientific view of the world, or by reflective knowledge of the original and inwardly necessary conditions of all being. As the mere will, taken by itself, is selfishly blind, and only receives by means of thought a guiding eye and the law of its action, so humanity has to be trained out of a one-sided practical attitude to a free and open sense of the original law and order of all being, which are based on the very nature of reality." There is no reason to think that we humans are the only immortal spirits in the universe, or even that this planet was created only for our sakes. Such ideas are obviously mere survivals of a cosmology which has long been abandoned, or creations of an overweening arrogance. To go back to them is not only to condemn ourselves to a distorted view of the universe, but to forgo a line of thought which has a great religious value, as widening our conceptions of God and abasing our high thoughts about ourselves.

It is difficult, I know, to criticise a one-sided view without falling into disproportion on the other side. In pleading for a juster estimate of the place of intellect in religion, I have no wish to disparage the part played in it by the will, or the aesthetic faculty. Spinoza identifies will and intellect, and this is better than to separate them entirely. We are not bound to arrange our faculties in order of merit, or to derive one from another. The only reason why the intellect must, in a sense, hold the highest place is that it includes the others - an intellectual judgment is the most complete act of the human mind. The simplest and most rudimentary psychical activity seems to be pure impulse, in which the agent neither wills consciously nor thinks. The second is the stage of will, properly so called, in which we know what we want, but not why we want it. The third and highest is the stage of reflection or intelligence, in which we know the "why" as well as the "what." Feeling and will are not absorbed or suppressed in the exercise of our highest mental activity, but they are disciplined and controlled by being brought into subjection to the realities which are outside of and independent of our wills. The difference between an educated and an uneducated man consists chiefly in this, that the educated man is guided by his intellect, the uneducated driven up and down by his wishes and feelings. It is the intellect which enables us to take the wide world's view of things. Heraclitus said that those who are awake have one world, but dreamers have each a world to himself. Among all the perverse judgments in Mr. Benjamin Kidd's book, none is stranger than his thesis that the intellect divides men, while the will unites them. Reason is not the private property of the individual, nor can it exist except as the concomitant of sociality. "Man would not be rational or human, if he were isolated," says Fichte quite truly.

This line of argument may bring cold comfort to those who are perplexed by what seem to them the irreconcilable contradictions between science and dogmatic theology. But let us consider the matter in another light. The fundamental postulate of religious faith is that no *value* is ever lost from the world. In whatever way we envisage the heavenly as opposed to the earthly, the perfect as opposed to the imperfect, whether we represent it under the form of time or place or substance, the eternal and spiritual world is God's treasure-house of all that shares in His nature and fulfils His will. The dread of religion when menaced by criticism, whether scientific or philosophical, is always lest some of its values should be invalidated. Science (using the word in the most comprehensive sense, for the study of fact, of whatever kind) is bound to set this consideration on one side, or rather it knows only one value, namely, truth. "It is quite true," says A. E. Taylor, "that logic is not the only game at which it interests mankind to play; but when you have once sat down to the game, you must play it according to its own rules, and not those of some other. If you neglect this caution, you will most likely produce something which is neither sound metaphysics nor sound ethics." Religion cannot accept as absolutely true any system in which the demands of the moral consciousness remain unsatisfied, and it has a right to point out that this or that generalisation based on scientific knowledge does not satisfy the moral sense. But to do this is to state a problem, not to solve it. The business of religion is, as I have said, not with values apart from facts, nor with facts apart from values, but with the relation between them; and it proceeds on the conviction that whatever is real is rational and good. The critical understanding cannot invalidate values, but only the forms in which they are enshrined, compelling a fresh presentation of them. When religious values are stated and interpreted in terms of fact, the critical understanding has the right to be heard. And similarly, the moral sense has the right to overhaul naturalistic ethics, though not naturalistic physics. It is plain, therefore, that no critical results can touch religious values, but only the casket in which they are enshrined. Whatever has value in God's sight is safe for evermore; and we are safe in so far as we attach ourselves to what is precious in His eyes.

In mystical theology, as I have said, we are often exhorted to get rid of the will altogether by laying it at the feet of God. "Those who accept all that the Lord sends as the very best," says Eckhart, "remain always in perfect peace, for in them God's will has become their will. This is incomparably better than for our will to become God's will."

Nothing can be more dangerous, if we may trust these experienced guides in the spiritual life, than to seek only satisfaction in religion, or to choose those doctrines and practices which give us most comfort, and suit our own idiosyncrasy best. When Suso asked a holy man, who came to him in a vision after his death, what religious exercise was at once the most painful and the most efficacious, he was told that no discipline is so sharp or so valuable as to be forsaken of God; for then a man gives up his own will, and submits, in obedience to the will of God, to be robbed even of his God. From the mystical point of view, this entire suppression of our wills is not the beginning of an aimless drifting, but the very contrary. For he who has given up his own will becomes the instrument of God's will, he becomes (as Eckhart says) to God what a man's hand is to a man. Those who adopt a rigid theory of personality cannot think of the matter in this way. The utmost to which they can aspire is, it would seem, a complete ethical harmony between God's will and our own. But this is not the experience which the saints have described for us; and it would not satisfy them at all. There is no room in the universe for more than one will, existing in its own right. Our approach to the likeness of God is not an approximation to a copy of God. It is rather a transmutation of our personality into a state in which God can think and will and act freely *through* us, unimpeded by any wilfulness on our part. No doubt it is the same experience which is described by one Christian as a surrender of his will to God, and by another as a vigorous assertion of his will as a worker or combatant on God's side. But one description may be more correct than the other; and there can be no doubt that it is the former which best corresponds with what the saints have told us about their own experiences. If they allow the human will any independent action, it is in the simple will towards sanctification, which, as St. Paul says, is "the will of God." In this sense Ruysbroek says, "Ye are as holy as ye truly will to be holy." But this must be taken in connection with other passages, in which the writer inculcates the complete surrender of the will. The essential point is that the motive power is not in ourselves. We cannot even will to please God without the help of His will. The experiences of the saints, as recorded by themselves, offer no support to a voluntaristic psychology of religion.

"No age of the world was ever strong, except when faith and reason went hand in hand, and when man's practical ideals were also his surest truths." [3] Faith and reason both claim jurisdiction over man's whole nature, and therefore no delimitation of territory between them is possible. The present distrust of thought as a way to religious truth must be a transitory phase. The spirit of the age, as I have said, is against it. This is a positive, constructive age; we are in earnest about our religion, but we are in earnest about our science too. We are not likely to abandon the right to seek God's truth in external nature, nor our hope of finding it. We are not likely to abandon the great discovery of the nineteenth century, the close relationship of human life with all other life in the universe, and the resulting cosmocentric view of reality. We are not likely to rest content with Lotze's theory of a world of human spirits, independent enough to produce even "surprises for God," as Professor James suggests, in the midst of a world which has no real existence and no real significance. Of all ways of "cutting the world in two with a hatchet," this attempt to separate man from his environment is surely the most unsatisfactory. It only seems possible because we have not yet fully realised all the implications of the great scientific discoveries in the last century. It takes a very long time for a great discovery to produce all the readjustments which it ultimately makes inevitable. It may be doubted whether even Galileo's discovery has yet been fully assimilated in popular theology or in ordinary thought. If so, it may be a long time yet before it is realised that any philosophical or religious theory which separates man from nature - which draws an impassable line anywhere across the field of existence, whether the line be drawn at self-consciousness or consciousness, or anywhere else is untenable. Even the distinction between living and dead matter, with which Drummond makes so much play in his clever attempt to find Calvinism in biology, is now felt to be of very dubious validity. It is, I believe, mainly because many are unwilling to accept this conclusion, preferring to kick against the pricks in the hope of escaping from it, that this theory of an irreducible dualism between value and existence is just now so popular.

For my own part, I cannot see that Christianity, or any spiritual religion, is threatened by the adoption of a cosmocentric view of reality. It no doubt commits us to the doctrine, which has from time to time been maintained in the Church, that if there are any other spiritual beings in the universe besides ourselves - and there is an overwhelming probability that there are many - Christ must redeem them as He has redeemed mankind. It also lends a new force to the "hope" which even St. Paul, with his limited knowledge of nature's secrets, entertained: that "the creation may one day be delivered from the bondage of corruption into the glorious liberty of the sons of God." In so far as organisms less highly endowed than our own partake of life and spirit, they can hardly be excluded from the sphere of values which we believe to be indestructible. I believe that the doctrine that Nature is in various degrees animated and spiritual throughout, is destined to gain ground. It is viewed favourably by Lotze, who, however, fails completely to reconcile it with his doctrine of personality, and is defended more consistently by Fechner, whose *Tagesansicht* and *Zendavesta* deserve to be much better known to English readers than they are. It is the logical development of the Logos-doctrine of the Alexandrians on its cosmological side.

Christian eschatology is not disturbed by this theory more than it has already been disturbed by the destruction of the geocentric hypothesis. We must frankly admit that much of our traditional language about heaven and hell was taken over from prae-Christian beliefs, and has now only a symbolic value. The ancient picture of the world, as a three-storeyed structure, is accepted in words both in the Old and New Testament; and has manifestly affected such descriptions as that of the Ascension and the Second Coming of Christ. Of course, it was recognised, even in antiquity, by thoughtful persons that such expressions as above and beneath, heaven and earth, were metaphors; just as Plato in the seventh book of the *Republic* says: "It makes no difference whether a person stares stupidly at the sky, or down upon the ground. So long as his attention is directed to objects of sense, his soul is looking downwards, not upwards." For a long time the local and spatial symbols were regarded as literally true, concurrently with the spiritual doctrine that God is everywhere, and heaven wherever He is. St. Augustine did much to legitimise the spiritual doctrine, which is no afterthought, no explaining away of dogmatic truth. "God," he says, "is present everywhere in His entirety, and yet is nowhere (*ubique totus et nusquam locorum*). He dwells in the depths of my being, more inward than my innermost self, and higher than my highest (*interior intimo meo, superior summo meo*). He is above my soul, but not in the same way in which the heaven is above the earth." So the scholastic mystics say that God has His centre everywhere, His circumference nowhere. Abelard says that though the Ascension of Christ was a literal fact, we are not to believe that the body of Christ now occupies a local position. The material ascension was only a picture-lesson of the "better ascension" in the souls of Christians. This attempt to combine the material and the spiritual was made more difficult by the destruction of the geocentric theory, and there is now great, and perhaps inevitable, confusion of mind among Christians on the whole subject. The Roman Catholic Church still teaches not only that the purgatorial fire is material, but that it is situated in the middle of the earth; but it is certain that educated Romanists do not believe this. We cannot cast stones at them, for in our Church the teaching about the Ascension is equally chaotic. The story of a literal flight through the air is still treasured by many people, though we have all, I suppose, abandoned the idea of a geographical heaven, which alone gave to it a coherent meaning.

The question of *time* in relation to eschatology is even more perplexing than that of place. To Eastern thought, time is an illusory movement, leading to no result. Reality is stationary. This fallacy, which deprives life of any rational or moral meaning, was escaped, at least in theory, by the Neoplatonists and their Christian disciples. Plotinus realises that "Νοῦς is everywhere" - that it must be at once σπάσις and κίνησις, rest and motion, and he never intended his Absolute to represent mere stationariness. Time, as Professor Royce says, is the form of the will. It is fulfilled, not in stationariness nor in infinite duration, but in achieved purpose. But this achievement cannot be attained at any point of time, for time itself is always hurling its own products into the past. Therefore, to quote Boethius, who puts the matter as clearly as any later writer: "Whatever suffers the condition of tune, even though it never began to be, and should never cease to be, yet it cannot be called eternal. For it does not comprehend and embrace the whole at once; it has lost yesterday, and has not yet gained to-morrow." "Eternity," says Eckhart, "is a present *now,* which knows nothing of time. The day of a thousand years ago is not further from eternity than the hour in which I stand here." All that we call duration implies a comparison of two or more different experiences, any one of which may be chosen to measure the rest by. Absolute duration could only apply to a Being who is *all* in *all* its experiences. The outcome of such thoughts is that to achieve immortality is to have life more abundantly, to be eternal in every moment. "He to whom time is as eternity, and eternity as time, is free from all stress," says Jacob Boehme. We experience a thing just in proportion as we are *in* it and make it our own. And interest in its highest power is love. Whosoever, therefore, loves God, abideth for ever.

This principle will prevent us from regarding any period of time, any experience, as merely a means to something beyond itself. To separate entirely means from end is one of the commonest and worst errors in religious philosophy, and indeed in practical life also. Work without enjoyment, and enjoyment without work, are both evil, and it is evil to make either of them our ideal picture of the soul's journey or its goal. Eternity is neither the sphere of mere continuance, nor of mere reward and punishment. It is the sphere in which all values are preserved, freed from the changes and chances of mortal life; and therefore eternity is our heart's true home. To sum up, if in our teaching we make the truth of Christianity depend upon a view of reality which satisfies the claims of Praxis, but leaves the claims of Gnosis the best Gnosis available in our generation utterly disregarded, we cannot expect, and we ought not to wish, that our message will be welcomed. Christianity has been a philosophical religion from the time when it first began to have a sacred literature. It claims to be the one explanation of life as we know it, an explanation to which heart and head and will all contribute. In order to understand it, we must act out our thoughts, and think out our acts; we must know ourselves, and we must know the world around us, if we wish to know God, who made both, and in whom both have their being. It is in the interplay and frequent collision of Gnosis and Praxis that sparks are struck out which illuminate the dark places of reality. The problems are difficult. Of course they are! Do they not range over earth and heaven and hell? But assuredly those who, in the vigorous phrase of one of the Cambridge Platonists, have made their intellectual faculties "Gibeonites," hewers of wood and drawers of water - those who have made no effort to "add to their faith knowledge," will never reach the perfection to which God called them, nor know Him *quem nosse vivere, cui servire regnare est.*

[1] Herrmann, *Metaphysics in Theology.*
[2] *Parerga and Paralipomena,* vol. ii.
[3] Professor H. Jones, in *Hibbert Journal,* January 1903.

Six - The Problem of Sin

A horror of sin is at the root of every vigorous religious creed. The opposition of good and evil, which from the moral standpoint is radical and irreducible, must be fully recognised in religion, unless religion is to be sublimated into a theosophy, or degraded into ritual, cultus, and magic. The most serious charge, therefore, which can be brought against any type of religious belief is that it promotes moral indifference. This charge has been frequently brought against mysticism, at any rate of the intellectual, philosophic type, though it is not possible to bring it against the great mystics individually. Since, then, I have undertaken in these lectures to defend the Christian Platonism which is the close ally of mysticism, I can hardly avoid attempting to grapple with this difficult question and considering briefly the great problem of Sin. The subject is, of course, far too large for one lecture. I can only indicate some aspects of the problem, and the direction in which, from the standpoint adopted in these lectures, we must look for a solution.

For the sociologist there is no problem of sin. Ethics, from his point of view, arose out of co-operative action. Primitive man discovered that he needed his fellow-inan to help him to realise his ends. At first, perhaps, it was a combination of purely self-seeking units. Then, when no coherence was attainable in this way, the germ of ethics became instinctive obedience to a rule, without reference to the immediate advantage of individuals. We may observe a stereotyped example of such a system in the polity of the bee or the ant. Theirs is a fully organised, or rather mechanised life, a sinless life, in which, so far as we can see, no one kicks over the traces. The hive is a society in which the same round of tasks is discharged in the same way from generation to generation; a stationary condition in which there is no ideal unrealised, aspired to, or rejected. Why is the history of mankind unlike that of the little busy bee, and the ant who is an example to the sluggard? Apparently because from a very early date man began to use his wits to evade or lighten his labours, to aggrandise himself, and in one way or another to alter his condition to what seemed to him a better. The possibility of progress and of retrogression came to him together. He chose to place himself on an inclined plane, with almost infinite possibilities of improvement and of degradation. And all through his life, if he attempts to rise, he has to resist the dragging force of the old animal nature, in which his ancestors lived so long. He has risen above himself, though without leaving himself. And he has lost for ever the ability to lead the purely animal life. That stage he has cast behind him, though the desire for it is not dead. If he gives up the struggle to be a man and tries to live as an animal, his doom is to become not an animal but an idiot or a devil.

There is no problem of evil here. We cannot eat our cake and have it. We may envy the ant or the bee or the wolf or the tiger, but nature has made us men, with special faculties and special disabilities. We must accept our lot, for better or for worse.

Neither is there any problem of evil for the moralist. Morality tries to destroy evil, not to account for it. Morality accepts a state of war, it strives only for victory. If morality were the whole of religion that religion would be Manicheism. Religion would be service in the army of Ormazd against Ahriman.

But morality is not the whole of religion, and for religion there is a problem of sin. There must be a problem, because for religion the "ought to be" both is and is not. God is not God unless He is all in all, but the God of religion is not all in all. This looks like an irreconcilable contradiction at the very heart of religion. It cannot be overcome by making the time-process an ultimate reality, and assuming an actual progress towards the realisation of God's will in the universe. For a God who has not yet come into His own is no God. We cannot suppose that God will ever have any more power than He has now, or that He has advanced from a condition of impotence to the dubious and divided sovereignty which he now appears to exercise. Science, too, knows nothing of such an universal progress, and will have none of it. Every organisation, large or small, every individual and every species, has its own law of growth and decay. Its destiny is to realise the idea which God formed of it in His mind and then to disappear from phenomenal existence. This is as true of a world as of a fly. Perpetual progress, as a religion, is a pathetic illusion. Perfection belongs not to any condition to be actualised in the future, but to the timeless whole.

The most real thing within our experience is what is sometimes called the kingdom of values, but, as I should prefer to say, of laws, which make up the content of the mind of God. These laws *are* reality. In time and place this means that they energise and fulfil themselves. So we can rightly pray, "Thy will be done on earth as it is in Heaven." Among these laws or values is the law which binds us to a life-long struggle with what in the time-series appears as evil. This law of struggle for the good constitutes the chief value of life in this world. As Plotinus says: "Our striving is after good, and our turning away is from evil: and purposive thought is of good and evil, *and this is a good*." Undoubtedly moral goodness implies a turning away from evil as well as a striving after good, and therefore (to quote Plotinus again) if any one were to say that evil has absolutely no existence, he must do away with good at the same time, and leave us with no object to strive after. The conflict between good and evil belongs to life in time. Eckhart is perfectly right in saying that "goodness" cannot be correctly predicated of the Godhead, who is above time. There is, of course, a difference between super-moral and non-moral. God is not neutral between goodness and badness, nor is His nature compounded of the two. For since evil is inwardly self-discordant and self-destructive, and rebellious against the law of the whole, its inclusion in the will of God means its complete transmutation and suppression in its character as evil. Sin (of which death is the symbol though not the punishment) is the last enemy that shall be destroyed. Viewed under the form of time, figuratively, the complete victory over sin will be the termination of the world-order, the end of the "reign," the distinct activities, of the Son, as St. Paul says. It is plain that morality is entirely occupied in striving to abolish the condition and object of its own existence. For, unless evil had at least a relative existence as evil, there could be no morality. Evil is thus in a sense a cause, as being a necessary antecedent condition, of good, and if so, it cannot be radically bad. "Things solely evil," says St. Augustine, "could never exist, for even those natures which are vitiated by an evil will, so far as they are vitiated, are evil, but so far as they are natures they are good," [1] or, as Plotinus says "vice is always human, being mixed with something contrary to itself." This is not to be confounded with the view of Buddhism, in which evil is the true kernel of existence, only to be removed with the cessation of existence itself. We believe that all that is good is preserved in the eternal world, but not the evils which called it forth. For that which is not only manifold but discordant cannot exist, as such, in the life of God.

The teaching about sin in Christian theology has been from the very first confused and inconsistent. Even St. Paul wavers between the Rabbinical doctrine of Adam's transgression as the cause of human sinfulness, and the very different theory, also held by Jewish theologians, that the ground of sin is in our fleshly nature. From the first century downwards Christian teaching about ski has fluctuated according as dogmatic, philosophical, or ethical interests held the foremost place. St. Augustine regards evil as a fundamentally perverted will, which proceeds from the free guilt of Adam; so that all men are a mass of corruption and only the predestined can be saved. The difficulties raised by this theory are fairly obvious. Besides the objections (not strongly felt until recently) against the hypothesis of an original perfect state, how could Adam have been tempted if his will was purely good? If we assume an innate predisposition to evil, we must find another origin for evil before the overt transgression which only brought it into the light. To throw back the problem into the world of spirits by introducing an external tempter is obviously no solution. And besides, how should Adam's sin infect all his descendants? The patristic idea seems to have been that all future generations were actually part of Adam at the time when he sinned. "We were in the loins of Adam," says St. Augustine. But the logical conclusion from this would seem to be not that we are guilty of Adam's transgression, but that he is guilty of all ours.

Into this mass of contradictions a purely aesthetic view, which he borrowed from Greek philosophy, oddly intrudes itself. "As the beauty of a picture is enhanced by wellmanaged shadows, so to the eye that has skill to discern it the universe is beautified even by sinners, though considered by themselves their deformity is a sad blemish." [2]

In short, St. Augustine's writings provide us with admirable examples of nearly all the incompatible theories about evil which have been propounded by thinking men; and the fact that his acute intellect dallies with them all in turn illustrates the extreme difficulty of the problem.

Contemporary theology generally adopts the theory of a perverted will, without the exaggeration of "total depravity," [3] though some have objected that if free will is the cause of evil, it must also be the cause of good, and that this is Pelagianism.

Others have felt that it is treating sin, as we know it, too tragically to say that it is essentially a revolt of the will against God. Such language appears absurd when we apply it to the delinquencies of children, or indeed to most of the faults of which we ourselves are conscious. Sin in its beginnings is no more rebellion against God than virtue is "resistance to the cosmic process," as Huxley suggests. It is only when selfishness has been accepted as a principle of action both by the intellect and by the will, that the word "rebellion" is appropriate.

The kindred definition, that sin is lawlessness which has the sanction of St. John is more instructive. Schleiermacher, indeed, objects that the law only prohibits acts, not states. But the law may and should be regarded as the moral idea in an imperative form. Thus Lactantius calls Christ *viva praesensque lex.* In the moral sphere the distinction between law and morality does not exist. But until we know what the law is, which it is the essence of sin to contravene, this definition does not help us forward much.

Another popular theory of sin, which is often set against the theory that sin is rebellion, is that which identifies it with *imperfection*. To the biologist evil (not "sin," a word which has no place in his vocabulary) is imperfection. In theology, this question has been one of the battle-grounds between Catholicism and Protestantism. Bellarmine and other Catholics distinguish between perfection and sinlessness, while Protestants have maintained that *omne minus Ionum habet rationem mali*. This involves the admission that perpetual progress in good involves perpetual continuance in evil. And if, with Fichte, we hold that life is a *progressus ad infinitum*, it would seem to follow that we can never be rid of sin. Perhaps under the form of time this conclusion cannot be avoided. Moral good is inconceivable without its antithesis, for without its antithesis it would be reduced to inactivity, and we cannot imagine that there will ever be a time when the moral sense could say, My task is done. But in a healthy development, nothing need be lost of the contents of the developing being. At each moment in our spiritual ascent, so far as we are really advancing, we answer to the claim which duty makes upon us at that moment. But this response, which is all that is needed for uninterrupted progress, is not incompatible with the presence of much which needs to be purified and transmuted before we can realise the will of God in and for us. Duty is the determinate moral requirement made upon a given individual at a given moment of time.

Something has been already said on the doctrine of original sin, connected by orthodox theology with the fall of Adam. The difficulties and contradictions of the traditional doctrine in this form have been well brought out by Mr. Tennant, in his recent Hulsean Lectures. But the story of the Fall is not the origin of the belief. "Original sin, the corruption of man's heart," is affirmed by human experience. It has never been asserted more strongly than by Byron, who did not pretend to speak as a theologian:

> "Our life is a false nature - 'tis not in
>   The harmony of things - this hard decree,
>   This uneradicable taint of sin,
>   Whose root is earth, whose leaves and branches be
>   The skies which rain their plagues on man like dew -
>   Disease, death, bondage - all the woes we see
>   And worse, the woes we see not - which throb through
>   The immedicable soul, with heartaches ever new." [4]

When the moral consciousness awakes, it finds within itself a strong tendency to lawlessness, which it cannot account for, and the source of which is plainly racial rather than personal. Whether the cause of the trouble is the Fall or the ascent of man from an earlier condition, the state of sin in ourselves is prior to self-consciousness, and has been inherited not acquired. Thus the doctrine which our modern poets have defended so eloquently has a real psychological basis, quite independent of any theological dogmas.

It may be worthwhile to inquire whether the confusion which we have found to exist about sin has been promoted by any disturbing influences which we can now trace. There can be no doubt that the supposed necessity for accepting the story of the Fall of man as literal history, has had a great influence upon Christian theology, though, as Bishop Gore said in a recent sermon, it has had singularly little effect on the rest of the Old Testament; while in the New Testament it is made the basis of an argument only in two chapters (Rom. v. and 1 Cor. xv.). The narrative in Genesis is indeed far more sober than some comments upon it. South's words that "an Aristotle was but the rubbish of an Adam, and Athens but the rudiments of Paradise," cannot be defended from the Bible. But there is no use in blinking the fact that we have to choose between the biblical and the scientific account of the early history of mankind; and I think it is impossible to maintain that the belief in a momentous lapse from virtue on the part of our first parents has been doctrinally inoperative. Many other primitive races have had their legends about a golden age in the past, when men were perfect and exempt from sin, disease, and death; but the notion would not have survived among civilised societies but for the idea that it has been guaranteed by Divine revelation. The unfortunate notion that pain and death are punishments for man's transgression comes from the same source, and has contributed to create a morbid feeling about both, and especially about death, which is common among professing Christians, but quite out of correspondence with the teaching of Christ.

The attitude of Christian theology towards sin is, on the whole, so much more gloomy than anything that we find in our Lord's teaching, that some cause must be found for the change. Christ Himself hardly mentions sin, except in connection with repentance and forgiveness. He never encourages either brooding over our past sins or self-imposed expiatory suffering. We hear nothing of the sense of alienation from God in His teaching, though it appears that He passed through this terrible experience for a brief moment on the Cross. Our Lord's teaching is very severe and exacting, but fundamentally happy and joyous. "The world" - human society as it organises itself apart from God - is to be renounced inwardly, but no war is declared against the ordinary sources of human happiness. On the contrary, the sufficiency of these simple natural joys, when consecrated by love and obedience to God, to make life happy, was part of His good news. But it seems to be the fate of great discoveries or revelations that the reconciliation which they announce is too profound to be understood, and they fall apart into dualisms. Plato's ideas met with this fate, and so, in a measure, did the greater teaching of Jesus Christ. I have suggested that the exceptionally severe mental struggles of such pioneers as St. Paul, St. Augustine, and Martin Luther may have had something to do with the exaggerations about human depravity, and the terrible struggle entailed upon all mankind against the mighty forces of evil. The average experience does not endorse this description of a continual and severe tension. We may admit this without having much belief in Professor James' "sky-blue souls," whom the devil appears to have forgotten. We all have our hard battle to fight against temptation. But I do not think that this battle, with most of us, has such a tragic and terrific aspect as Christian divines often describe; and I believe that if we took our tone more from our Lord's own words, and from the proportion observed in His teaching, we should get rid of certain exaggerations which to some appear distressing and to others unreal. I will even go so far as to say that we should sometimes resist, and check by our reason, those fits of intense self-reproach which are a common experience of the devotional life. These feelings move in great rhythms - persons of a nervous and emotional temperament are now exalted to heaven and now thrust down to hell. The recluse especially, of whom it may be said, as of Parnell's "Hermit," that "Prayer [is] all his business, all his pleasure praise," suffers these fluctuations of feeling in their fullest severity. But the man who is leading a normal active life ought not to do so; and the expressions, whether of union or of alienation, which a Suso or a John of the Cross could utter honestly would certainly not be wholesome, and would probably be unreal, in the mouth of an ordinary good Christian. In our experience, the conflict in the world is more often between the worse and the better than between the good and the utterly bad; and not infrequently the struggle in our own souls is between two goods, one of which is higher than the other, rather than between God and the devil.

Another disturbing influence has been the tendency of Christian moralists to fix their attention too much on the avoidance of sin and too little on the production of moral values. There has been a general tendency to ask what a man is bad for rather than what he is good for, Self-examination has concerned itself more with the deadly sins than with the cardinal or the theological virtues. Some of the Platonising theologians, notably Clement of Alexandria, are free from this tendency; they feel, and say, that our object is not to be without sin, but to follow Christ. But, on the whole, sin has occupied a larger place in Christian ethics than virtue. This was not our Lord's own method; it is rather a return to the language of the old dispensation, with its long catalogue of things forbidden. In our time there has been a very strong reaction against it. "The modern man," said Sir Oliver Lodge the other day, "is not worrying about his sins at all." If he is not, he ought to be; but not to the extent advocated in some of our most popular devotional manuals. The servants in the parable were asked what they had to show for their talents, not how they had spent their play-time.

There are then special circumstances which have complicated a problem already difficult enough. Christian theology has not been able to make up its mind whether sin is a defect, or a transgression, or a rebellion, or a constitutional hereditary taint, or whether it is all these combined. The same degree of uncertainty is shown when the question has to be answered, What is the characteristic form of sin? What is the root-principle to which all sin may be reduced? To this question at least three answers have been given. The root of sin is sensuality - is pride - is selfishness. To the Greeks, indeed, none of these answers seemed so satisfactory as the theory that the source of sin is delusion or disease - a perverted condition of the mind. This answer, which brings one aspect of the truth into prominence, has been unduly neglected in Christian theology. Matthew Arnold was quite justified in saying that in England at any rate people are far too much absorbed in the effort to walk by the light which they have, forgetting very often to make sure that the light within them is not darkness.

The theory that the root of sin is sensuality is favoured by St. Paul in some passages, though he does not really regard "the flesh," still less "nature," or "the body," as the seat of the evil principle. No one who held this latter view could pray, as he does, that we may be delivered from all defilements of the flesh and *spirit*. St. Augustine says very well: "It was not the corruptible flesh that made the soul sinful, but the sinful soul that made the flesh corrupt." [5] The theory that "the corruptible body presseth down the soul" is often supposed to be the doctrine of Platonism. The truth is, that it was taught as an exoteric theory by the later Platonists, and was readily accepted by disciples whose cast of thought was of the oriental type; but it is not true Platonism, and has never satisfied the great thinkers of this school. In modern times, this view of sin has found but little support. Rothe is the chief exception. He combines selfishness and sensuality as a double root of sin, but leans, on the whole, to the view that sensuality is the primary cause. But to find the root of sin in sensuality is to materialise religion, and sins of sensuality were not those to which Christ attached most importance.

Pride is certainly the most naked form of sin; for pride is self-deification. It may be madness or disease, it may be rebellion, but inasmuch as it claims to be a law to itself, it is the very principle of sin come to self-consciousness. Augustine and Thomas Aquinas both say that pride is the beginning of sin, though not its root. We might equally well say that it is the *end* of sin, its completed development in self-chosen independence of God.

Those who have found the root of sin in selfishness or self-will have best understood both the teaching of Christ and the nature of sin. We find the theory clearly stated in Plato's *Laws* (v. 731): "The truth is that the cause of all sins in every person and every instance is excessive self-love." This declaration is somewhat isolated in Plato, and was perhaps the conclusion of his later years. In his earlier works we find the better-known figure of the unruly chariot-steeds, and the picture of the disorderly passions struggling for mastery, or falling under the dominion of a master-passion. Philo finds the root of sin in selfishness (φιλαυτία), and when we turn to the New Testament we can hardly fail to see that this is the leading conception. In the deeply significant parable of the Prodigal Son, the beginning of the prodigal's downfall is his request, "Give me the portion of goods that falleth to me." Again and again our Lord declares that His Divine mission consists in this, that He is not come to do His own will, but the will of Him that sent Him. Again and again, both in the Gospels and in the Epistles, the truth is inculcated that we must die completely to self, forget, and starve, and crucify self, before we can enter the kingdom of God. A man cannot be a disciple of Christ unless he *hates* (so hyperbolical is the language in which our Lord sometimes couches His deepest teaching) not only all his possessions and worldly ties, but *"his own soul also."*

It would be impossible to find stronger words to express that self-consciousness, self-seeking, self-indulgence, selfishness in all its forms, is the root of sin. The mystics, as we might expect, accept this teaching with their whole hearts. It has now fallen somewhat into the background, under the influence of modern individualism, of which our so-called socialism is often only a frantic variety, and it naturally meets with no favour from the school of personal idealists. The gospel of self-abnegation has not been much favoured by the European races in modern times, either in principle or practice. We have been wont to contrast complacently our own energetic self-assertion with what we call the dreamy pantheism of Asia, and have pointed to the subjugation of the contemplative Oriental by the vigorous European as a testimony to the superiority of our religion and philosophy. God, we like to say, helps those who help themselves. This Deuteronomic religion, which just now suits the temper of the Germans even better than that of the English, will perhaps soon cease to appear satisfactory to either nation, and may give away also on this side of the Atlantic. The time may be coming when we shall see a little more clearly the limitations of our favourite theories and practices. Civilisation based on individualism has defaced or destroyed much of the natural beauty of the globe; it has made life more difficult than it ever was before, and it now shows signs of breaking up from within. The gigantic aggregations of capital on one side, and the growing hosts of unemployed and discontented on the other, are a *reductio ad absurdum* of the whole system which cannot be disregarded. Hardly less significant is the nervous overstrain caused by modern competitive business, which in the great centres of population, where the struggle is most intense, seems to be actually sterilising many families, and leaving the world to be peopled by inferior stocks. And now, amid these disquieting symptoms, we see the emergence into power of the Japanese, whose whole morality is based on the self-sacrifice of the individual to his country, who live the simple life, and who set the smallest possible value on the preservation of their own individual existence. Those who have thought that Providence has definitely handed over the sceptre of the world to races of European descent, and especially to the representatives of robust Teutonic individualism, are probably destined to have a rude awakening. The late war in the Far East is an object-lesson which can hardly be thrown away upon Europe and America.

Sin, then, according to the view here adopted, shows itself in self-consciousness, self-will, and self-seeking. Self-consciousness, instead of being the proud privilege which gives us a special rank in the hierarchy of God's creatures, is the blot on our lives which spoils all that we do. Even in games, if nervousness causes us to think about the stroke which we are trying to execute, and which at other times we perform mechanically, we are almost sure to do it badly. In social intercourse, self-consciousness is destructive of good manners. In religion it leads to spiritual [valetudinarianism, or to what is called priggishness. It has half spoiled many saintly characters, giving their virtues a stiff and forced appearance, which falls short of the true beauty of holiness. Whether the Pharisee thanks God that he is not like the publican, or whether the publican thanks God that he is a humble Christian, not like the Pharisee, in either case he will return to his house without a blessing on his prayers.

As for selfishness, how wonderfully science has reinforced Christian precept on this subject! Everywhere in nature we see the individual sacrificing himself in the interests of the race. In many species of insects the act of procreation itself involves the immediate death of one of the parents. Yet these duties are not shirked. That nature is careless of the single life was observed long ago by Tennyson; and assuredly the sovereign rights of the individual are not contained in her charter. Schopenhauer saw clearly enough that Nature's purpose is not the greatest happiness of the isolated individual, and that all her baits and traps are designed to induce the individual to sacrifice himself in one way or another. This recognition must issue in pessimism, just so long as we determine to stick to our impervious monads, our self-existing individuals, the subjects of indefeasible rights. But the true conclusion is not pessimism. It is only the conviction that since there are in the nature of things no self-existing units with these rights and privileges, selfishness is a ruinous mistake, a blunder which leads to shipwreck in all parts of Nature alike. For Nature cannot be disobeyed and outwitted with impunity. It is our wisdom to obey cheerfully, with the clear consciousness that we are not allowed to work out our own salvation as isolated units, and that obedience will involve us in pain and loss, perhaps irremediable loss. For our obedience must be, in will if not in deed, obedience unto death, even the death of the cross. Vicarious suffering, which on the individualist theory seems so monstrous and unjust as to throw a shadow on the character of God, is easy to understand if we give up our individualism. It is a necessity. For the sinner cannot suffer for his own healing, precisely because he is a sinner. The troubles which he brings on himself cannot heal his wounds. Redemption must be vicarious; it must be wrought by the suffering of the just for the unjust. And the redemption wrought by One is efficacious for many, because we are united to Him by closer bonds than those of ethical harmony. Sin is that which cuts us off from all this. It erects an image of the false self, the isolated, empirical self, which has no existence, and makes this idol its god. The forms of worship which are offered to it differ greatly. The false self may be pampered and indulged, or it may be treated as a hard taskmaster, and slaved for day and night. Huge quantities of gold and silver may be stored up for its future use, as if it was to live for ever; or lastly, as savages break an idol to which they have prayed in vain, the false self may be punished by killing the body to which it is attached; disappointed selfishness may end in suicide.

Here, then, is a view of sin which gives us a practical standard. As the *Theologia Germanica* says, it is in the I, Mine, Thou, and Thine that all evil has its source. Does this view demand an impossible detachment from personal, living interests? It seems to me that it does just the opposite. We are what we are most deeply interested in. We are what we love. And what we love, because we love it, is not external or alien to ourselves. "Amate quod eritis," says St. Augustine. Outside interests are only outside because we make them so. In the spiritual world there is no outside or inside, no mine and not mine; all is ours that we can make our own. All is ours if we are Christ's. For Christ, as the Logos, the Power of God, and the Wisdom of God, is the life of all that lives, and the light of all that shines. Is it not always just that fatal reference to our own interests that cramps our sympathies, warps our activities, and blinds our perceptions? The self-seeking man may do good social service by accident, as it were, as the condition of receiving a reward which he considers worth his while. But he is always potentially an enemy of society. He can only be utilised as long as society is willing to pay his price. A society of self-seeking units is always liable to go to pieces, since it is held together by a purely artificial or accidental bond. In reality no road has ever been found, or ever will be found, from "each for self" to "each for all." Our civilisation is at present worked on the calculation that motives are mixed. It relies upon material rewards and punishments, upon praise and blame, and upon moral and religious sanctions. The disappearance of any one of these three classes of incentives would wreck the whole social machine. But this is not an ideal state of things. And it is worth observing that the selfishness which is so potent a social lever is not for the most part undiluted selfishness. Even the mere money-spinner, if he attains to any sort of distinction in his pursuit, must be a sort of idealist, a sort of artist; and art, even in its least exalted forms, is a nobler thing than selfishness; it has an universal element in it. No one could be an artist who took account only of what helped or baffled him personally, neglecting all else. "Art," it has been said, "is the wide world's memory of things."

The loss of faith in eternal life seems to be the just nemesis of individualism. It is instructive and rather pathetic to see how some of the school which I have mainly been criticising in these lectures turn to such "evidence" for survival after death as has been collected by Mr. Frederick Myers. One would have supposed that this kind of immortality - in which we apparently show our continued activity only by occasionally terrifying our surviving friends - would have had no attractions for any one. And one would have supposed that men who have had some experience of human credulity and self-deception would have disdained to dabble in spiritualism. But the individualist, who has staked everything on his own self-existent personality, who can hardly think of immortality except as survival in time (time being to him absolutely real), and who is puzzled to say how immortality thus conceived can be the destiny of mankind, really needs evidence of this sort; and since no good evidence is forthcoming, he must be content with bad. Many others, as the *questionnaires* lately circulated in America and England have proved, "have the courage to say that they do not desire this kind of personal survival in time. I have no space to discuss doctrines of immortality, or to show what an amazing medley of incompatible theories lies concealed behind the popular eschatology. This much is certain, that if the "impervious ego" can ever and anywhere succeed in realising himself, it can only be in hell. A kingdom of heaven inhabited by a population of spiritual monads, the number of which is determined by the fluctuations in the birth-rate and the duration of human life on this planet, or, as Anselm and others believed, by the amount of the accommodation available in heaven after the expulsion of the fallen angels, is hardly credible except as a symbolical picture. If we once realise that dreams of a heaven in which *we* ourselves are the centre are a transference to the eternal world of those selfish schemes and imaginings which are the essence of sin, we should put them away from us, and thereby remove from our path the chief stumbling-block in the way of belief in our eternal destiny. Our personal life has a meaning and a value; that value and that meaning are eternal; there is no danger of their being ever lost. Still less is there any danger of love ever perishing for want of its object. Love is divine, and implies immortality. Nor should we ever forget that we are deciding by our lives here our rank in the eternal world. But the Christian eschatology, avowedly symbolical as it is, becomes grotesque and incredible symbolism if we transfer to heaven and hell the crude notions of individuality which for the most part pass unchallenged in the West.

I think we may claim that the religious philosophy of the mystics gives us a practical standard of right and wrong, while it removes some formidable stumbling-blocks from our path as Christian believers. It does not solve the religious problem of evil, nor does it pretend to do so. That problem has been stated once for all in the words of Augustine: "Either God is unwilling to abolish evil, or He is unable: if He is unwilling, He is not good; if he is unable, He is not omnipotent." No Christian can consent to impale himself on either horn of this dilemma. If God is not perfectly good, and also perfectly powerful, He is not God. It has indeed been argued lately by some Christian thinkers, such as Dr. Kashdall, that God is not omnipotent. Such a conclusion does credit to the consistency of a philosopher who is before all things a moralist; but it is so impossible to any religious man who is not defending a thesis, that it only serves to illustrate the weakness of the premises which led to such a conclusion. The only other alternative, if we refuse St. Augustine's dilemma, is to deny, to some degree, the absolute existence of evil, regarding it as an appearance incidental to the actualisation of moral purpose as vital activity. And in spite of the powerful objections which have been brought against this view, in spite of the real risk of seeming to attenuate, in theory, the malignant potency of sin, I believe that this is the theory which presents the fewest difficulties. I do not think that it ought to weaken us, in the slightest degree, in our struggle with temptation. For sin, as a positive fact, is as real as time is real, and as free will. We may still say, with Julian of Norwich, "To me was shown no harder hell than ski."

In these lectures I have undertaken the defence of one recognised type of Christian thought, which may be traced back through the more philosophical of the mystics to the Christian Platonists of Alexandria, and through them to St. Paul and St. John, The obstacles in the way of such a faith, in which I myself have found happiness and satisfaction, seem to me to be (1) a needless distrust of the intellectual processes as a means of arriving at divine truth, leading to the sceptical conclusion that, since the truth is for ever hidden from our eyes, we may believe whatever seems to help us; and (2) a neglect of the doctrine of the mystical union with the glorified Christ, which seems to me at once the most blessed and the most *verifiable* part of the Christian revelation. This is why I have talked so much about theories of personality, and about the anti-intellectualist trend of much modern philosophy and theology. There is too much sceptical orthodoxy just now; and orthodoxy based on scepticism is unsound and hollow. An imperfect faith which is sure of essentials is better than a faith which will accept everything because it recognises no standard of truth except human needs. I know that there are unsolved difficulties; I feel them myself. I do not think that the difficulty about miracles will be solved in our generation. But I feel sure that the path of wisdom for most of us is to look forward and not back - to leave purely historical problems alone for the present, and to learn to know and love Christ as He can be known and loved by us in the twentieth century in Europe and America. This, combined with patient and reverent study of the laws of nature, is the way to the true enlightenment which will lead us step by step to the love of God, the perfect love which casteth out fear.

[1] *De Civ. Dei,* xii. 3.
[2] *De Civ. Dei,* ii. 23.
[3] S. T. Coleridge, while rejecting the theory of transmitted guilt, assumes an universal and timeless act of self-degradation in the will of the human race a theory which is as incomprehensible as the patristic one.
[4] *Childe Harold,* iv., 126.
[5] *De. Civ. Dei,* xiv. 2, 3.